designs & plantings for
conservatories
sunrooms & garden rooms

designs & plantings for
conservatories
sunrooms & garden rooms

inspirational ideas, planning advice and planting information, lavishly
illustrated with more than 300 stunning photographs and artworks

DIANA YAKELEY

WITH PHOTOGRAPHY BY CAROLINE ARBER

aqua marine

This edition is published by Aquamarine,
an imprint of Anness Publishing Ltd, Hermes House,
88–89 Blackfriars Road, London SE1 8HA;
tel. 020 7401 2077; fax 020 7633 9499

www.aquamarinebooks.com;
www.annesspublishing.com

Anness Publishing has a new picture agency outlet
for images for publishing, promotions or advertising.
Please visit our website www.practicalpictures.com for
more information.

UK agent: The Manning Partnership Ltd;
tel. 01225 478444; fax 01225 478440;
sales@manning-partnership.co.uk

UK distributor: Grantham Book Services Ltd;
tel. 01476 541080; fax 01476 541061;
orders@gbs.tbs-ltd.co.uk

North American agent/distributor:
National Book Network;
tel. 301 459 3366; fax 301 429 5746;
www.nbnbooks.com

Australian agent/distributor:
Pan Macmillan Australia;
tel. 1300 135 113; fax 1300 135 103;
customer.service@macmillan.com.au

New Zealand agent/distributor: David Bateman Ltd;
tel. (09) 415 7664; fax (09) 415 8892

Publisher: Joanna Lorenz
Senior Editor: Lucy Doncaster
Designer: Pink Stripe Design
Illustrator: Jane Hudson
Editorial Reader: Penelope Goodare
Production Controller: Claire Rae

© Anness Publishing Ltd 2009

Ethical Trading Policy

Because of our ongoing ecological investment
programme, you, as our customer, can have the
pleasure and reassurance of knowing that a tree is
being cultivated on your behalf to naturally replace
the materials used to make the book you are holding.
For further information about this scheme, go to
www.annesspublishing.com/trees

Publisher's Note

Although the advice and information in this book are
believed to be accurate and true at the time of going to
press, neither the author nor the publisher can accept
any legal responsiblity or liability for any errors or
omissions that may be made nor for any inaccuracies nor
for any harm or injury that comes about from following
instructions or advice in this book. The plans on the Case
Study pages are not intended as architectural elevations.

Picture Credits

The publishers would like to thank the following for
permission to reproduce their images (t=top, b=bottom,
l=left, r=right, m=main, c=centre):
Alamy 8–9m; 10cl; 13tr; 18tl; 20tl; 21bl; 62bl; 63br; 142bmr.
Amino/Apropos Tectonic 27m; 33br.
Anness Publishing Ltd 35tr. The item of furniture is
available from Parma Lilac, 98 Chesterton Road, London,
W10 6EP; (parmalilac@aol.com); 52–53 The architects of
this conservatory are Yakeley Associates Ltd; 64–65 The
architects of this conservatory are Rick Mather Architects.
Carol Sharp Studio 95tr.
Corbis 7tl; 11tr; 13bl; 15br; 16tl; 34br; 44bl; 55bl; 55br.
Diana Yakeley 14tr.
EWA Stock 6bl; 15tr; 24cl; 25bl; 58tl; 61tr; 63cl; 77tr;
80m; 81br; 90bl; 97br; 101br.
Garden World Images 20br; 47t; 69tr; 107tr; 109tr;
112tl; 129br.
iStockphoto 1; 12tl; 57m; 75tr; 91m; 97tr; 106tr; 115br;
136bl; 136cl; 140tr; 141br; 142br; 143tl; 144tml; 144tl;
145bmr; 146br; 147tr; 154bmr; 155tml; 155tr.
O ECOTEXTILES 94tr.
Photolibrary Group 7br; 12cl; 19bl; 19br; 45m; 54m; 63tr;
71tl; 92bl; 92br; 93t; 104t; 106bl; 108tl; 114bl; 115tr.
Prêt-à-pot 96cl.
Silent Gliss 89m.
Taylor Howes Designs 88bl.
Vale Garden Houses 14bl; 16cl; 17tr; 21tr; 22–3m; 25tl;
25tr; 29t; 32m; 46m; 56bl; 59tl; 60bl; 66–7m; 68bl; 70bl;
72bl; 73tr; 73br; 75br; 79m; 82tl; 86–7m; 94b; 100bl.

Contents

introduction

The pursuit of the rare and exotic has long been an obsession of gardeners, and the ability to bring light and space into buildings has intrigued architects from the Roman period onwards. The combination of the two interests has produced some glorious structures both in the public and the domestic domain, where conservatories continue to be popular.

Light is vital to the well-being of our planet and the plants and animals living on it. Essential for growth and spiritual health, without sunlight humans can become ill and depressed, so it is natural for us to seek as much light as possible to enable us to work as well as simply to relax and absorb sunlight on our skins. There is something wonderful, therefore, about being in a structure made almost entirely of glass. To be protected from the elements and yet have uninterrupted views of the sky and the natural world outside in a controlled climate is one of the great achievements of modern technology.

Throughout the ages there have been a variety of different names for glass structures that provide shelter for plants, from orangeries and greenhouses to sunrooms, conservatories and porches. The term 'greenhouse' usually refers to a functional place devoted solely to growing plants. Orangeries, structures originally designed for growing citrus fruits in cold climates, are generally of a more solid construction of brick or stone, with high arched windows which could be opened to allow the plants to be wheeled outside for the summer. The domestic conservatory, on the other hand, has evolved as a largely glazed structure attached to at least one wall or forming part of the house, which is used both for living and for growing plants.

A conservatory can be integrated into an existing house relatively easily, providing an extra room that can serve as part of a kitchen, dining or living room, flooded with pure light; a useful transition from house to garden. Using modern construction methods it can

incorporate heating, lighting and ventilation to enable year-round use, and range in style from wildly nostalgic reproductions from a bygone era to seamless glass boxes. The availability of large sheets of glass has made it possible to radically alter existing properties by removing walls or roofs and replacing them with large glass panels with minimum impact on the architecture, making old buildings more versatile and in keeping with modern lifestyles.

In an increasingly urbanized and crowded world, these imaginative spaces often become the most used areas of our homes, sheltered from the elements yet visually connected to the outside. The purpose of this book is to look at conservatories, sunrooms and garden rooms as additional living spaces that may or may not include plants, although it will be hard to resist growing something organic, green and beautiful in these inspiring structures.

OPPOSITE This lovely period conservatory fulfils a dual purpose, providing year-round sanctuary and room to grow for a range of plants, and a tranquil, beautiful setting for a special meal.

RIGHT A sensitively designed glass extension to a terraced house creates a new light-filled room in a previously unused space to the side of the house without clashing with the period style of the building.

chapter one

getting started

The Victorians understood the romantic draw of the conservatory. Assignations were arranged behind the potted palms and an interest in the latest horticultural finds was a perfect excuse for an uninterrupted dalliance. Today's uses are numerous but the appeal of a profusion of scents and harmonious colours still provides a life-enhancing experience. There are many factors that need considering before you start planning a glass structure, and this chapter provides an overview of the process, as well as an insight into their evolution and history.

LEFT Soft green tones make this conservatory an irresistible place in which to unwind. The lush planting both inside and outside helps create a transition from one space to another.

evolution and history

From the ingenious heated shelters of Roman times to the cutting-edge buildings of today, conservatories have undergone many transformations over the centuries. In addition to their original horticultural purpose, modern glass structures are also used in different ways.

ABOVE This 15th-century painting by Pietro de Crescenzi shows gardening in a *hortus conclusus*, an enclosed garden. The walled garden gave both protection for plants and a secluded place for people to enjoy the pleasures of outdoor life.

The conservatory as we know it today owes much to the ebullient Victorian period in Britain, although the principle of providing shelter for tender plants goes back to the Roman era, when the health benefits of eating fruit and vegetables were first becoming recognized. The need to keep these tender plants warm produced an array of ingenious engineering solutions, from using thin sheets of mica to form a cover to tapping the heat produced by fermenting manure in trenches, or introducing warm air through ducts built into walls.

Although the invention of glass is believed to have been achieved by the Syrians in around 5000BC, it was the Romans who began to use glass for architectural purposes around AD100, following the discovery that by adding manganese oxide to carbonate of sodium and silica they could make clear glass. Cast glass windows, albeit with poor optical qualities, thus began to appear in the most important buildings in Rome and the most luxurious villas of Herculaneum and Pompeii. The fall of the Roman Empire, however, slowed down the development of glass techniques and it was not until the 13th century that the production of small pieces of sheet glass began.

During the Middle Ages, the cultivation of decorative plants was mainly limited to the aristocracy, who were the only ones who could afford to plant and grow them. These were often planted in a *hortus conclusus* or enclosed garden, designed to protect privacy and to keep out animals and unwanted visitors. These walled gardens were the only alternative to the modern garden shelter until later in 15th-century Italy, when structures linking the house to the landscape, such as pergolas and covered walkways, became fashionable.

The Renaissance

A period of great change and innovation, the Renaissance heralded the arrival of new, exotic fruits in the West. Of these, oranges, lemons, limes and pomegranates were the most sought after, both for their medicinal properties and for their scent and flowers. Early Italian gardeners quickly learned to protect them during cold winters by moving them into specially built shelters called *Limonaiacan*, or lemon houses. These symmetrical small buildings can still be seen in some Italian villas, where they fulfil their original role.

The use of plant shelters in formal Italian Renaissance gardens prompted the northern European aristocracy to create bigger and better versions of the *Limonaiacan*, where exotic fruit could be grown despite the harsher northern climate of extreme cold and plentiful rain that combined to thwart their plans. Called orangeries, these were elegant buildings with long glazed openings where plants in containers could be rolled out during the warmer times of the year, leaving the space free for banquets at other times. A magnificent example of this can be seen at the Château de Versailles, on the outskirts of Paris, and it was here that Versailles planters were invented. These wooden structures had fixtures to allow poles to be inserted on each side, which enabled two men to carry the sizeable lemon or orange trees out on to the terrace in mild weather.

The Industrial Revolution

Throughout the Renaissance period conservatories were very much the preserve of the aristocracy. It was not until the advent of the Industrial Revolution, when glass, cast iron and wrought iron could be manufactured on an affordable scale and the tax on glass was rescinded, that the domestic conservatory came of age.

The Industrial Revolution was a time of great progress, invention and exploration. In addition to new technologies, there was a huge influx of new plants, brought back from around the world by plant hunters.

ABOVE The magnificent orangerie at the Château de Versailles, where tender plants thrived indoors during the cold winter months before being brought on to terraces after winter frosts had passed.

LEFT The need to protect citrus fruits, prized for their health-giving properties and aromatic scent, led to the construction of specialized glass shelters during the Renaissance. Today, these plants remain popular conservatory species.

TOP The Palm House at Kew
Gardens, by Decimus Burton,
was designed to accommodate
the crowns of palm trees.

ABOVE 'The Luncheon in the
Conservatory' by Louise
Abbema, 1877. A prosperous
family group, including the
actress Sarah Bernhardt, enjoy a
new informality in a conservatory,
amid luxuriant foliage.

This combination of an increased interest in exotic plants and the advances made by the pioneering engineers of the Victorian era produced some of the most spectacular glass structures for growing plants anywhere in the world. The names of John Loudon, Decimus Burton and Joseph Paxton are synonymous with the development of the great conservatories, working with engineers and foundries to create these innovative pavilions.

Early designers of these structures were often plantsmen first, and designers second. Joseph Paxton, head gardener to the Duke of Devonshire at Chatsworth house, is said to have been inspired by the delicate tracery on the undersides of giant water lilies' structurally strong leaves to design the Great Conservatory or 'Great Stove', built in 1836 to house the Duke's renowned plant collection, which was, at the time, the largest glass building in the world. Something of a polymath, he went on to design the massive Crystal Palace in 1851 for the Great Exhibition at the height of the Victorian era and later became Member of Parliament for Coventry. Decimus Burton also collaborated with Paxton on the Chatsworth conservatory, and his work survives at the Royal Botanic Gardens, Kew. The dramatic Palm House is one of the most inspiring and impressive glass buildings ever built, and the Temperate House, completed after his death, remains the world's largest ornamental glasshouse.

The technology developed for these imposing structures of glass, wrought or cast iron and wood could be adapted to cover any large spaces such as railway stations, shopping arcades and exhibition halls and many examples from this age survive today, of which Paddington and St Pancras Stations in London and the Galleria Vittorio Emanuelle in Milan are fine examples.

The 20th century onwards

Two world wars took a toll on many of the privately owned conservatories, as the costs of upkeep became too much and manpower was limited. The 'Great Stove' at Chatsworth was one of those to suffer and, having been neglected, unloved and unheated for the war years, it was demolished in 1920. Five explosions were needed to destroy the noble structure, which proved to be a symbolic end to the golden age of conservatories.

A new era in architecture was, however, emerging in 20th-century Europe as the Bauhaus school in Germany sought to develop a new architectural style to reflect a new age, combining art and industry to produce rational and functional buildings. One of the most important architects to come out of this period was Ludwig Mies van der Rohe, who fled Germany in 1937 and settled in America, and whose work with steel and glass has transformed the way buildings in cities throughout the world look today. His sublime Farnsworth House, built in Illinois in 1951, allows clear views of its woodland setting through uninterrupted glass walls and would still be thought of as avant garde today.

Another of the 20th century's most famous residential buildings is Philip Johnson's Glass House in Connecticut. Inspired by Mies van der Rohe, this exquisite glass box sits serenely in its landscape, blurring the boundaries between house and nature.

At the forefront of glasshouse design in the late 1950s was the Climatron. Created for the Missouri Botanical Garden, this monumental geodesic dome was designed by St Louis architects Murphy and Mackey on the principles of Buckminster Fuller, who designed the first geodesic dome and showed that not all conservatories needed to be rectilinear. The Climatron has no columns from floor to ceiling, allowing more light and space for tall palms. This structure paved the way for modern architects, who are now able to produce increasingly complex curving glass structures with solar control properties and immense strength.

In addition to the innovation in design, advances in glass manufacture and double glazing now make it possible to produce glass that will reduce heat gain or loss, filter ultraviolet rays, be self-cleaning, become opaque at the flick of a switch, resist bullets, provide heating, or encapsulate LED lights. Any of these features can be incorporated into the planning of your conservatory – the only limit is one's imagination and budget.

ABOVE Farnsworth House in Illinois was built by Mies van der Rohe, one of the key figures in the development of steel and glass structures in the 20th century.

LEFT The Climatron at the Missouri Botanic Garden was a geodesic dome made from a network of triangular sections of glass.

things to consider

Modern conservatories have many uses, from garden rooms and spaces to relax in, to offices and kitchens. With so many factors to take into account, good planning at the design stage

RIGHT Conservatories need not be at ground level, as this one demonstrates. Planning permission is often required, especially if you share an outside wall, and good communication throughout the process will help things go smoothly.

BELOW Muted blue tones unite this garden and conservatory, creating an irresistible sanctuary. Using the same floor tiles inside and out creates a seamless transition.

As with all projects involving building work it is important to be very clear about what you wish to achieve, what your realistic budget is and what hidden costs need to be allowed for. Planning permission may well be required depending on where you live and whether you (or the previous owner) have used up your permitted extension allowance, particularly if you live in a conservation area or a listed building. Regulations ensure that the building is safe in terms of structure and fire risk and meets environmental concerns about heat gain, heat loss and fuel consumption. Legislation and building regulations change from time to time so always check with your local authority before starting work, or seek advice from a qualified architect. In most countries building regulations apply to energy ratings for windows and the conservation of fuel and power, and can be downloaded from the internet. Local authorities have the power to require you to take down your structure if you ignore any of these planning requirements or regulations, so it is very important to be well informed before starting work.

If you share an outside wall with your neighbours, as is common in many cities, you may need to seek party wall agreement if you wish to use the shared wall as part of your conservatory. There are costs attached to obtaining these permissions, so these need to be factored into your budget at the outset.

Talk to your neighbours at the start of the project and show them what you are considering. Involving them at early stages of the design is not only considerate, but may well lessen the chances of them objecting to your planning notice at a later stage, when costs have already been incurred. Disputes between neighbours can become heated and bitter, so are well worth avoiding wherever possible.

For very large conservatories of over 30m/100ft above ground level, building regulations will apply and your local authority should be able to advise on how to comply with them. It is often possible to have informal talks with your planning department who may give some indication of what they will allow and more importantly what they will not before you start.

Specialist conservatory manufacturers should also be able to advise on what is feasible and what needs to be done by them or by others, including you. Draw up a list of all your options, which should include the following considerations.

Aspect and orientation

There may be a limit to the choice of site for the conservatory, but the orientation of the new room is one of the most important factors to be considered. There may be only one obvious place, usually at the back of a property, leading to the garden and accessible from a living room or kitchen. For those in the city, rooftop extensions offer a chance to create a light-filled extra space, giving views over the urban landscape or simply bringing light into dark stairwells. Side infills at ground floor level, often adjacent to a kitchen, are a popular way of bringing overhead light into dark terraces and glazed extensions across the whole of the rear façade are often more acceptable to planning departments than extending into the roof for extra living space.

A sun-filled room will be perfect for growing tropical exotics, but not so good if you have a collection of shade-loving ferns or valuable antique furniture.

ABOVE All the woodwork and furniture has been painted the same colour to contrast with the walls in this conservatory. This helps create a sense of space in a small room.

RIGHT The owners of this house have the advantage of an idyllic year-round view for their conservatory and can watch the changing seasons and observe the local wildlife.

TOP Receiving sun late in the day, this simple conservatory is perfect for a late lunch or afternoon tea, or just admiring the sunset.

ABOVE A good designer will advise on a wide range of options for windows and materials. The better the quality, the lower will be your future repair costs.

Take into account that good ventilation will be essential in a glazed extension that receives a lot of sun, as will the provision of blinds or special glass to keep temperatures down during summer. Conservatories that get morning sun are ideal as breakfast rooms, whereas one that receives afternoon sun will be perfect for an afternoon and early evening drink, as well as providing ideal conditions for more exotic plants. Shadier structures are cooler and better for temperate plants, provide insulation to the coldest wall of the house, and have the quality of light much prized by artists. Glazed roofs will allow a surprising amount of light even on the most overcast day, and can transform even the darkest rooms. This question of aspect will be constrained by the layout of the house, but affects the cost and use considerably.

Financial considerations

Always go for the best quality your budget will allow. Planning carefully in advance saves expensive additions at a later date, which could have knock-on effects on work already completed. Weigh up the initial costs of more expensive options, which may be cheaper to maintain in the long run. Double glazing is good at reducing sound and you should even consider triple glazing. This may cost more, but it will be more secure and will have better thermal properties, which will lower running costs dramatically. Likewise underfloor heating, which often costs less to run as the heat is evenly distributed and can be run at a lower temperature. Other forms of heating may take up usable wall or floor space, will affect where furniture or plants can be placed, and may look intrusive.

Nothing is less conducive to the enjoyment of a room than having to look at a detail which could have been done better – all that bright light will show every imperfection. Employing an expert conservatory designer or architect to help you will produce a well-considered and individual scheme. Always allow a contingency sum for unforeseen problems – there usually are some, especially where older existing buildings are involved. There are a great many companies offering conservatories, some more design-led than others. For a conservatory to be both complementary to the house and suitable for your exact requirements requires a dialogue between manufacturer and client. You should expect to see sketches of the proposed design and the way it relates to the house, as well as working drawings for the final plan. Listen carefully to what the designer suggests – it may not be what you had envisaged but they are the experts and have past experience behind them as well as fresh ideas – but don't be afraid to ask questions if you are not sure what you are being shown. You are the client, so be sure that you are being given exactly what you want. Understanding the details as fully as possible from the start will help you to be sure of this, and also enable you to monitor the work's progress more carefully and spot any problems.

Materials

The level of maintenance required to keep a conservatory in good order will very much depend on the design of the conservatory and the material used to hold the glass in place. Traditional conservatories were made with wrought iron or timber glazing bars but few of these exist now except in botanic institutions and stately homes. Timber is often the choice of bespoke fabricators, but will need to be regularly treated or repainted; the sections are often a little heavier in appearance than aluminium, but will look so much better with the traditional timber window and door frames of older properties.

Even the most basic structure will need good foundations, ideally laid at the same level as those of the house. Check that any garden trees are as far away as possible, a minimum of 3m/10ft or up to 30m/100ft (depending on the variety of tree) to prevent damage to the foundations and to glass; glass doesn't like movement. Taking out a large tree can also cause problems, especially on clay soil, causing movement, or heave, to any nearby structures. Your local authority should be able to give advice on garden trees, and whether you are permitted to take them out in the first place. Planning permission will be needed if the tree is of a certain size.

Access from an existing house to the conservatory also needs careful thought. It may simply mean using an existing door or dropping the sill of a window, but it could well involve taking out walls and inserting supporting lintels – a much more specialist undertaking.

ABOVE A fine traditional conservatory where no expense has been spared to produce a structure that will add to the value of the house. Sympathetic materials have been chosen to match the house, and the terrace and landscaping have been carefully created to make a harmonious design.

Innovations in glass technology are making glass a versatile and practical building material. Advances in tougher, safer glass with greatly improved thermal qualities are producing buildings of great beauty and transparency. Our desire for more open-plan living in rooms that have a variety of uses is driving the manufacture of technically advanced types of glass and will eventually bring the costs down.

With more emphasis being placed on 'green' choices, the use of photovoltaic cells to harness the sun's energy for heating might be considered. Major glass manufacturers are now able to produce glass that is self-cleaning, possesses excellent thermal qualities for both solar gain and loss, and is immensely strong – an important safety and security aspect. Initially high costs might prove a good investment in the long run, so research your options and discuss them with your conservatory builder. Think about the benefits of mechanical ventilation to cool the conservatory (or alternatively to heat it), and weigh them against the

ABOVE The need to conserve energy has led many architects to use the latest technology when designing new homes. Photovoltaic cells and solar panels, shown above, are incorporated in some new developments. You should be aware, however, that the initial cost of using this technology is high at present and may take many years to recoup in reduced fuel bills.

financial outlay. In a world threatened by climate change, the costs of traditional heating fuels may soon become prohibitive, and solar or geothermal power could become the norm.

Impact on the house and garden

Adding an extra living space may increase the value of your home, but only if it is done sympathetically, competently and is well maintained. There are many options to consider, from choosing a design that echoes the period details of the house to creating a modern seamless glass extension. When in doubt, keep it simple. Overly decorated designs may be harder to maintain – leaves may gather on complex roofs and window cleaning may become a chore if you have fiddly mullions or glazing bars. The beauty of glass is that it is transparent and allows other features to be seen so why complicate matters with bolt-on decoration?

The owners of one architecturally important house with a glazed roof-to-garden extension had to employ abseillers to clean the sticky residue from a nearby lime tree (with a preservation order) from the large amounts of sloping glass forming a new back wall of their property. A small price to pay for a ground-breaking and award-winning design, but one probably not thought of at the outset.

It is not advisable to construct conservatories that would restrict ladder access to the windows of rooms in roof or loft conversions, particularly if any of the windows are intended for escape or rescue if there is a fire. Again, if in doubt, consult your local authority for clarification on this. On older properties with low eaves, where it would be difficult to use the outside wall, it may be better to provide a glazed link between the house and the conservatory. This will enable the design to be read as a separate pavilion and is a useful way of connecting to larger structures such as pool houses, which might otherwise be out of scale with the original house.

BELOW LEFT Every aspect of this double-height conservatory has been carefully thought through. The table and chairs have been positioned so that they are not obstructive, and the beautiful staircase enhances the light, airy feel of the space.

BELOW RIGHT A traditional terraced house has been transformed by simply glazing over an otherwise awkward area.

The scale of the conservatory is an important factor in relation to the size of the house. The design should be in proportion to that of the property – too large and it will dominate the façade of the building, too small and it will look like an ill-conceived afterthought. Designers and architects will be able to show you drawings of how your design will look in relation to the property and explain the limitations of planning and building regulations on the scheme. They may also suggest design alternatives that you may not have considered.

A conservatory will also provide an extra layer of insulation to the wall of the property it is built against and eliminate draughts, but may well take some of the light reaching the original room inside, unless you plan to enlarge the opening between the two. It may well be worth considering doing this to open up the interior of the house, allow more light in and integrate the two rooms.

ABOVE This well-designed extension brings light in at high level and through concertina glass doors. A smooth transition between the family room and the sleek dark wood decking creates an outdoor living area in keeping with the interior design of the house. Architectural planting completes the picture.

RIGHT Evergreen shrubs such as box (*Buxus*) are ideal for the terrace and can be clipped and trained into sculptural shapes relatively easily. They prefer sun but are tolerant of some shade, and work well with both contemporary and traditional gardens. The choice of planter makes the difference.

Try to ensure that the transition from house to conservatory and conservatory to garden flows well. Well-chosen flooring and hard landscaping can help with this, making the new room look like an integral part of the house, rather than an ill-thought-out addition. Alignment of doors also should be carefully planned – placing internal doors opposite the new external doors can lead to a tunnel effect between furniture and affect the circulation of the space. Consider, too, the alignment with any garden features. It may be that you have a magnificent view already aligned with your chosen site, but it is more likely that you need to partly redesign the garden, creating a focal point by designing, say, a new path leading the eye to a feature, a tree or sculptural form. There is little point in building a wonderful new room only to then look out at a dense laurel hedge or a drainpipe. A paved or deck terrace makes a good transition to the garden and gives an area for dining or barbecues in summer, as well as providing a visual base for the conservatory extension and a place for some large sculptural pots and attractive planting.

Detailed planning

Designers map everything out on paper or computer to make sure there is enough room for any furniture and comfortable circulation, and that the proportions are pleasing. It would be sensible to do this for yourself using graph paper and a scale rule. Draw a plan of the proposed floor space, preferably at a scale of 1:20. Note where doors and windows will be and where you intend tables, chairs, storage and plants to be positioned, and allow enough circulation space around each piece. This enables precise positioning of power and lighting points in relation to the furniture arrangement, and helps when shopping for new furniture. Never make impulse buys when choosing large pieces of furniture and be prepared to measure everything meticulously – too many people have found to their cost that doors are too small to accommodate a large sofa or table or that it dominates the space if you do manage to squeeze it in successfully.

For those with growing families the use may change, from providing a safe place for young children to play, to accommodating a television and computer, or a place to do homework when they are older. Modern living patterns are flexible and changing and it is easier to provide for all possibilities in terms of power sockets and lighting during the building stage than to try and add them later. Kitchens, living and dining rooms are all good uses for the glazed extension; bedrooms and bathrooms less so, requiring more privacy and lighting control.

If the conservatory is to include plants, their needs will have to be given careful thought and included in the design process. Where the conservatory is primarily

for plants and where water is present, any sockets and electrical parts will need to have a waterproof rating – in the UK and the US this is known as IP56; in Australia it is IPX4 Waterproof or IPX7 Waterproof; and the Japanese Industrial Standard (JIS), a waterproof scale from 0 to 8 (0 being the least resistant) may be used in several countries. These safety codes must be observed and a good electrician will be able to tell you what they are.

All of these vital factors are considered in depth in the Practical Factors chapter, but it is important to be aware of them from the outset as they will affect how you plan your conservatory or sunroom.

ABOVE Modern living requires flexible spaces, and careful planning of wiring and furniture layout enables the conservatory extension to work well for a variety of uses. Good blinds are needed for viewing screens without glare, but need to be planned into the design at the initial stages of construction. Afterthoughts always add to the final cost.

LEFT Recessed floor sockets with stainless steel hinged covers look less obtrusive than standard sockets, and have dictated the width of the surround to this flooring design. Always check that waterproof rating safety codes are adhered to, especially if plants and water will be present in the room.

chapter two

different uses

The luxury of living in a house specifically designed for your personal needs is not an option for most people. Old properties often lack a light-filled, open space that can be used in a variety of different ways and at different times by all members of the family. You may require a family room where children can play and eat, a studio or office, a kitchen extension or simply a place to grow plants and watch the natural rhythm of the seasons from a warm and sheltered place. A simple conservatory can fulfil any of these functions at relatively low cost.

LEFT This conservatory is used both as a dining room and a place in which to relax. Good blinds help protect fabrics from bright sunlight, which would fade them.

a flexible space

None of us ever seem to have enough space – space to think or simply relax or space to work, play or socialize with our friends. A conservatory or sunroom can provide the solution to many problems and, whatever the weather, a way of enjoying the many and varied delights of plants in a controllable environment throughout the year.

Adding a conservatory or sunroom to a house is a relatively easy way of providing an extra room and can bring light into otherwise dingy areas, often to the rear of the property. For some, it is intended as part of the open–plan living area, for others it may provide a space for a specific use, just chilling out or simply for growing a range of tender plants in.

A conservatory room opens up all sorts of possibilities. For many, the need to expand the existing kitchen and living area and create a social hub in the property is the most important reason for adding on. This creates a flexible space for informal dining or for children to play safely while being watched from the kitchen, or just a wonderful place to sit and read. With many people now working from home the extra space can also provide room to spread out and work peacefully in light-filled surroundings, constantly reminded of the ever-changing cycle of the seasons outside. For those who love gardening, the chance to grow tender plants all year round, and bring on seedlings or grow fruit and vegetables can be irresistible, and the conservatory is also the perfect place to then relax and admire the results of your efforts.

ABOVE A pleasing symmetry, accentuated by access through the existing doors of the house, shows careful thought at the planning stage and makes for an inviting and relaxed space.

OPPOSITE High level conservatories or sunrooms can give wonderful views over the countryside or cityscape and can often be added to flat-roofed extensions.

One great way to use the space, if you have room, might involve a small swimming pool or jaccuzzi, and many conservatories are built to enable year-round swimming in lusciously planted surroundings. Condensation will be a major factor to be considered with large amounts of water, however, and good mechanical ventilation will be vital. There will also need to be room for plants and equipment, making it a much more costly venture. It's a big decision, so think carefully about what you want to achieve.

For the serious plant collector the conservatory will be designed around the needs of the plants, with the emphasis placed on regulating the heat gain and

providing essential ventilation. The design may also incorporate internal planting beds as well as staging for smaller plants, and watering systems can be installed and lighting positioned specifically for the benefit of the plants. All these factors will depend on the type of plants you wish to grow and the aspect of the conservatory. You should bear in mind, however, that a conservatory designed around the specialist needs of some plants may be too cool or humid for everyday living, so check plants' requirements before you buy them. Details of some species suitable for the conservatory can be found in the plant directory.

ABOVE LEFT The experience of dining in this delightful garden room surrounded by lush foliage and beautiful flowers will be transformed at night when scent fills the air and stars are seen in the sky.

ABOVE RIGHT The versatility of a garden room means that the space can be used for a wide variety of tasks and hobbies. Think about built-in storage at the planning stage to enable things to be put away safely and neatly. The soft green colour used here complements the colour in the landscape and creates a harmonious ambience.

a place to unwind

Living patterns have changed over the years, a fact that is not necessarily reflected in the layout of many older houses. A conservatory or sunroom, however small, will provide a bright, flexible and airy space that can bring in some much needed light to enhance our lives.

BELOW This cosy corner of a garden room provides a bolt hole and a relaxing space away from the rest of the house. With a comfortable sofa and soft cushions, even a personal sound system (but no telephone or other distractions from the outside world), it's a great place to unwind.

OPPOSITE A practical tiled floor combined with robust materials and furniture makes this colourful garden room the perfect place for family dining as well as plants, as it can be easily kept clean. Casual seating and ambient lighting make this a relaxed, informal place for a range of activities.

By far the most popular use of the contemporary conservatory is to create an informal family living area that fulfils several functions. An ideal place for small children to eat and play in, they work on all levels and for all ages, from the very young to the very old, who will appreciate the light, warmth, and close proximity to the rest of the household. The decision to use the conservatory as an extension to the living area will very much depend on the ease of access from either the kitchen or the existing living room or, even more practically, both. As kitchens are often at the rear of a property this is the most common area to link to or extend.

There are a number of factors to bear in mind when choosing furnishings for a living space. Large amounts of light will fade fine fabrics and wood finishes so it is important to choose both with care, and consider blinds for the sunniest time of the day. The light and contemporary nature of a largely glazed living area enables one to choose quite different materials and designs for furnishing this space compared to the rest of the home. Large upholstered pieces of furniture tend to look wrong, and lighter, more natural materials that relate to the outdoors are generally more suitable and do not interrupt the newly acquired view.

Venetian blinds or sliding panel blinds are a good choice for windows and will give you the option of controlling the amount of light without obscuring the view completely. Install plenty of power points and think about speakers for music; if you want them built in, it's best to incorporate this into your initial plan.

a place to work

Traditional home studies or offices tend to be small rooms that are not big enough for other uses, but how much more stimulating and less oppressive to work surrounded by a view of the outside and of the changing seasons, even in the heart of a city.

With more and more people working from home, a conservatory extension can create a perfect place to work. Garden rooms have long been the refuge for writers, artists and other creative people who benefit from good light and quiet spaces, and the advent of the internet and email have made it possible to do a much wider range of jobs without leaving home. The time spent commuting to work can be more profitably used working without the noise and interruptions of a traditional office atmosphere, in calm surroundings.

Those working on computers will need to control the daylight cast on screens by the use of blinds or shutters, and make sure that adequate power and phone points are in place. A few well-chosen aromatic plants will also serve to enhance the experience and blur the boundaries between house and garden.

BELOW Light and flexible, a conservatory can fulfil several functions. Here, a dining table doubles up as a temporary work space or area for homework. A desk lamp, which can quickly and easily be put away when the table is needed for other things, can be used when there is not enough light available from outside.

As the space may well need to accommodate other uses, careful thought will need to be given to the storage of valuable and important documents or computers. Simple, well-designed cupboards may be included in the design, or ottoman-like chests that could, with the addition of purpose-made cushions, double up as seats with storage underneath. Most conservatories have a brick dwarf wall as a base for the glazing system. The height of this, coupled with the depth of the sill, could provide an area to build understorage and provide an extra work surface at the same time, a consideration to be taken into account when planning the type of conservatory construction you choose. If your work demands privacy or you need a way of preventing distraction from the family, a door that can be closed from the main house would be worth considering. The space could double up as a quiet place for children to do homework in the evening or simply as a tranquil place to read and unwind.

ABOVE With good-quality, controllable blinds on the windows at all levels and solid office furniture, this uncluttered glazed extension makes an impressive place to work in at home. Carefully chosen paintings, indoor plants and tidy desk accessories add a note of relaxed formality, while views over the verdant garden provide inspiration and a sense of calm.

a place to dine

A conservatory that is close to or leading off the kitchen will provide the perfect place for eating informal family meals while enjoying uninterrupted views over the garden or terrace, and allow better interaction between family members or guests.

While formal dining rooms are becoming a thing of the past, there is still a need for a flexible space for everyday eating that can also accommodate larger gatherings. Dining under the stars, or being able to enjoy a view of the city or garden, is much more pleasurable than eating in a dark and formal dining room, and more in keeping with contemporary living. Having transparent glass walls puts more emphasis on the table itself, giving an opportunity to create imaginative table decorations for dinner parties or festive occasions.

As dining tables are large items of furniture, make sure you allow enough room for chairs to be moved in and out around the table comfortably, and do not prevent the circulation route to the door to the outside – measure everything carefully beforehand to ensure you achieve a well-designed space. Varnished wood or fine veneers will fade in bright sunlight, so a table of glass or stone, Corian or laminate would be a practical choice, as would a simple scrubbed wooden table stripped of any applied finish, depending on the sort of look you wish to achieve. Select dining chairs that are delicate and airy – blocking the view would rather defeat the object of having the light-filled space. Furniture that could be taken outside on to a terrace or lawn is a good option, and as the choice of well-designed garden furniture has widened, there is plenty to choose from.

Good lighting is important for everyday tasks but candles look wonderful at night, with sparkling reflections in the glass, especially when seen from the outside. With so many different tea light holders and candelabras available, the conservatory can be transformed into a magical space, especially if the garden is also lit sympathetically, blurring the transition between inside and out. A few attractive plants will also add to the setting, highlighting the link between inside and out and negating the need for short-lived cut flowers for special dinner parties.

ABOVE An unusual glass table looks right in this garden dining room, where the owners have introduced a strong oriental theme. Miniature bamboos echo this.

OPPOSITE Even on a dull winter day the quality of light in this conservatory lifts the spirits and makes a simple meal something special.

a place to cook

Contemporary kitchens often form part of the main living area in the home. The use of glass to open up the back wall of a kitchen with folding or sliding doors is now common practice and the technology for door systems and glazed roof lights is as sophisticated as your budget will allow.

Well-designed kitchens are one of the major selling points of one's home, so it can be a sound investment to dedicate a conservatory space to this usage. It is crucial that you take advice on the planning and construction of this type of conservatory, however. In addition to the safety aspects, it is likely that the room will be well used, so it is vital that you enjoy the detailing and efficiency of the design over many years.

Kitchens are steamy places at times, and since steam carries small particles of grease, thought will need to be given to the practicalities of cleaning glass at high level. Efficient mechanical ventilation will also be crucial. The choice of glass as a roof is of particular importance when using a conservatory as a kitchen space – too much heat gain in summer or too much heat loss in winter could make the room unusable. Using a Low E (Low Emissivity) coated glass will be essential here and self-cleaning glass will make cleaning from the outside almost unnecessary. Initial costs may seem high, but the benefits of lower maintenance in the long term may outweigh these. Self-cleaning glass only works on the exterior, unfortunately, the principle being that daylight breaks down dirt into tiny particles that are then easily washed away by rain, so you will still need to clean the glass inside the room.

Since kitchens are functional spaces and worktops are generally built in at around 90cm/3ft high, it is best to site units against solid walls or form islands in the centre of the room rather than against the glass. If you have room for a table, position that in the area left near the glass, but ensure access to the outside is not blocked.

Plants tend to like the warmth and occasional steam in kitchens, and benefit from the attention given by being constantly under one's gaze so you can spot any problems early. The immediacy of having fresh herbs or baby salad leaves growing nearby ready to snip as you need them is a great pleasure and a source of some wonderful scents.

OPPOSITE This extension provides a large open-plan kitchen and dining area, allowing the cook to interact with guests, or just enjoy the view of the garden in spacious, light-filled surroundings.

BELOW When the folding sliding doors of this kitchen are fully opened there is a seamless transition to the courtyard, making the space feel larger than it is.

a place for growth

Many conservatories are built simply as an additional living space, but it seems sad to ignore the origins of these glorious structures – as places for conserving rare and delicate or exotic plants – so it is well worth including a few plants, however small.

Apart from the obvious pleasure of being surrounded by beautiful and scented plants, there is a therapeutic element to any form of gardening that acts as an antidote to the stresses of modern life. A little knowledge about which plants are happy where and what their needs are, can develop into a passionate interest in the science of plant care, perhaps leading to travel to see plants in their native surroundings.

There is a huge range of plants available, so there is something suitable for every personality, from desert cacti to exotic bromeliads or colourful orchids. Good plants for conservatories can range from architectural palms and ferns to scented Mediterranean climbers, which create a lush tropical sanctuary in which to unwind. Sitting down and relaxing with the latest bulb catalogue or nursery plant list is a good opportunity to observe any problems with plants as well as to dream and plan what you will grow next year.

ABOVE Spring-flowering bulbs are easy to grow and provide colour and scent at the beginning of the year. Children can learn about the growth cycle by planting their own choice of bulbs and watching them bloom.

RIGHT A glorious profusion of aromatic plants compete for space with a fine old vine in this traditional conservatory, which is solely dedicated to plants. Old terracotta pots are artfully lined up on staging, showing the plants at their best, and water-filled cans provide humidity.

Most children love planting seeds and watching them grow, and the pleasure is even greater if the plants are scented and/or edible. Aromatic herbs such as basil or vervain and the tangy scent of growing tomatoes will remind one of summer picnics in a way that no store-bought packets ever will. Even more exotic are the scents of stephanotis, gardenias or jasmine, which produce beautiful blossoms at a time of year when most gardens are a little bleak.

Many people think that growing plants under glass is a difficult and specialist task. In fact, it can be as easy or as challenging as you like, depending on the plants you choose. It's up to you to decide how much time and effort you want to devote to their care, and select your plants accordingly. Access to the internet enables anyone to find out about the requirements of a particular plant or to buy their favourite species.

Successful integration of plants into the living space requires the careful choice of pots or containers. Nothing looks worse than a neglected conservatory used as an extra space for storing unhealthy plants and odd assortments of old garden furniture. Plastic pots may well be practical, but are generally not ornamental. They can, however, be placed inside a more attractive pot in keeping with other materials and colours used in the conservatory. Additional care needs to be taken if you do this to ensure that the plant is not overwatered, since ornamental pots may not have drainage holes – unless it thrives on having its roots in water.

Terracotta pots are practical for most plants but can look too rustic for chic conservatories. In the right setting, however, hand-thrown terracotta pots look wonderful and are certainly the best material for growing plants in, being both porous and well-draining.

There are also some elegant planters made from fibreglass with finishes that are indistinguishable from stone, copper, lead or stainless steel, and even leather. They have the advantage of being lightweight and, if used outdoors, frost-proof. One vine or palm can look far more dramatic in a well-chosen planter than a motley collection of disparate refugees from a plant sale.

ABOVE The elegant pineapple lily is particularly suited to a cool conservatory due to its long flowering period and interesting stems, leaves and complex flowers. This species requires light shade and regular watering.

LEFT Terracotta pots are ideal for conservatory plants as they are porous and well-draining. This vase shape would be pleasing in a country setting, but care should be taken to prevent surplus water from staining floors, and the narrow neck will make it difficult to remove plants for repotting.

CASE STUDY OF
a garden room

The desire to provide an environment in which beautiful, tender plants can be grown throughout the year dates back to the very first conservatories. The therapeutic benefits of tending plants are well known and there can be no place more conducive to completely unwinding than a scented room filled with exotic and glorious blooms.

This stunning conservatory perfectly demonstrates how lovely the original usage of the room, as a place for growing plants, can be. A profusion of healthy plants carefully chosen for their colour, scent and texture provide year-round pleasure in a sensitively designed conservatory that has been constructed in harmony with the main building.

The house, a fine 19th-century family home, has unusual period details, which the owner has carefully reproduced in the details of the conservatory. These include roof finials, floor tiles and stained glass panels. Built along the shady side of the house, the timber structure provides a link to a kitchen, study and drawing room, all accessed through delightful French doors, opening up the rooms to a light and scented space that is perfect for informal meals or as a quiet place to read and relax. In addition, siting the conservatory on a shady wall insulates the house against cold from the wind and reduces draughts to the living rooms.

OPPOSITE A profusion of lush green foliage and the graceful branches of an acacia frame the view outside in this lovely garden room. Mostly white flowers create a calm and elegant feel, enlivened by the occasional flash of a showy deep red bloom.

RIGHT Period details from the 19th-century house have been sensitively incorporated in the extended conservatory which sits beautifully in the landscape. Wild strawberries grow through the steps, and evergreeen shrubs blur the boundaries between inside and outside.

LEFT The soft bloom of a pelargonium leaf can be as beautiful as any flower. It has the added advantage of being scented and is believed to deter mosquitoes; especially important if the room is to be used as a place for relaxing as mosquitoes are never welcome.

LEFT Slatted staging allows plants to be moved to the fore when at their best and tucked away in a safe position when they are dormant. *Eucomis autumnalis* thrive in pots at floor level, masking the area beneath the staging.

BELOW Original timber finials found in an outhouse provide detailing consistent with the original house. White paint looks fresh and provides a good background for greenery.

BELOW *Pelargonium* 'Lord Bute' adds vibrant accent colour to an otherwise white and green colour scheme.

BELOW Different shades of subtle green enlivened with pure white flowers create a calm and elegant colour palette for the carefully chosen planting.

BELOW A delightful stained glass detail in the doors echoes those found elsewhere in the house and provides a suitably floral motif.

Designed primarily for the needs of plants, this lovely conservatory sits on a brick plinth wall, which enables staging to be placed at waist height, giving storage space for pots and watering cans below. Slatted staging also allows for good drainage from pots and air circulation around plants, which are important for preventing diseases such as mildew and rot. Planting at this level allows a good view of the plants when sitting, and also makes spotting insects or problems at an early stage easier.

In accordance with the cohesive nature of the internal and external design, the architectural detailing to the woodwork reflects that of the main structure. Dusty old pieces of finial found in an outhouse during the renovation have been reconstructed and painted, adding an authentic touch to the new building. Great care has also been taken to use handsome old terracotta pots and traditional Victorian red and black encaustic tiled flooring, completing the painstaking period detail.

Water is stored in a magnificent old vessel, allowing any sediment to settle and for it to reach room temperature before being used for watering. The water also provides a level of ambient humidity on which the surrounding plants thrive.

Although there is a profusion of lush green planting everywhere, a restrained palette of mainly white flowers is used, with the occasional deep red bloom providing accent colour. A mature and happy mimosa provides an overhead canopy, with twisting stems and abundant flowers completing the garden room.

TOP RIGHT These pots have been arranged so that the mass of plants can easily be watered and tended while still being clearly on view, providing the perfect backdrop for a relaxing moment in this lush garden room.

RIGHT An antique water container tucked in a corner provides a stylish and neat solution for water storage, giving humidity to the surrounding air as well as maintaining room-temperature water for the many plants.

CASE STUDY OF
a swimming room

Using a conservatory to house a pool is the ultimate luxury, and if done well creates an oasis of calm in which to swim and relax. As with all pools, however, there are obstacles with regard to maintenance issues and ventilation that need to be considered before you start planning.

BELOW The double height industrial structure of this conservatory is a dramatic setting for a private pool, surrounded by large-scale tropical planting. Raised planting beds allow for seasonal changes to the smaller plants at low level.

This spectacular pool conservatory is a conversion of a structure previously used for the commercial production of roses in the south of France. The double-height space gives the opportunity to grow large specimens of banana palms and other evergreen plants in conditions that allow them to gain the height and breadth normally impossible in a domestic conservatory.

Year-round swimming surrounded by such lush tropical planting is an extraordinary experience. Citrus trees, heavy with fruit even in winter, grow alongside bird of paradise flowers, and clash with shocking pink bougainvillea and pelargonium flowers. In this oasis of calm, scent is intense and adds to the feeling of being enclosed in an exotic private spa or secret garden.

An elegant and sheltered loggia leads from the house to the conservatory, where simple Tuscan columns support the arched openings and reflect the arched windows of the pool house. A neutral palette of buff and pale terracotta materials unites the different spaces and is also typical of the local vernacular.

Operable windows in a lantern structure keep the conservatory cool, the heat rising through the industrial space into the roof, the air kept moving by motorized fans. Lighting comes from simple plaster uplighters positioned at regular intervals between window bays and gives a cathedral-like glow to this tall space at night. Plants are grown in beds directly into the ground rather than in pots, and have been chosen for their scale or ability to scramble and climb the high walls. Scale is vital in this space as small plants would be lost by the sheer size of the space unless they are used, as here, as colourful infill ground cover. Plants grow well here due to the ideal mixture of light, warmth and humidity.

LEFT *Strelitzia regina* or bird of paradise flowers thrive in the light-filled and humid conditions here, and seem to be observing the swimmers.

BELOW Bougainvillea and citrus thrive in this Mediterranean climate, providing colour and scent.

ABOVE High-level fans with integral lighting circulate the air and help create a cooling draught.

BELOW This variegated rubber plant, *Ficus elastica* 'Doescheri', heightens the tropical feel of the room.

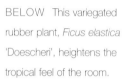

BELOW Architectural plants make a striking statement and give a lush, tropical feel to the planting.

ABOVE Pelargoniums are a good choice to add colour at low level below the jungle-like structural planting.

chapter three

choosing
the design

Our personal choices say a lot about who we are – traditional country lovers, urban minimalists, creative collectors of interesting bits and pieces or over-the-top drama queens. There is a bewildering selection of off-the-peg conservatories to suit every size, taste and budget, but will they be right for the style and shape of our property and the use we wish to put them to? Adding a conservatory is an expensive outlay and not one that can be discarded if we realize that high Gothic style isn't quite what we wanted, so it needs to be thought through.

LEFT Linking the kitchen to a dining area overlooking the garden is one of the most popular ways of using the consevatory extension, providing a very flexible open space.

different sizes and shapes

One of the most obvious limiting factors when considering a conservatory is the space available. Whether you have limitless room to expand or choose to creatively adapt an awkward corner, it is important to ensure that the inside space will be sufficient for your purposes.

BELOW If you only have space for a small conservatory, think carefully about what you want to use it for, and make sure your plans are realistic.

OPPOSITE This dining area has been successfully added to the side of a terraced property, linking well with the decked terrace and small garden.

For a successful project, it is important to achieve a good balance of scale and proportion, and it is this that will give you visual pleasure every time you use the new space. We tend to prefer symmetry and balance in all sorts of things, from faces to buildings, so bear this in mind when you are making your choices about the shape and size of room design, both inside and outside. A good designer or architect will be able to help achieve this.

It can be useful to photograph the façade of the building you wish to add to and to make copies on to which you can draw different shapes and sizes with a felt pen. Look carefully at existing details such as the angle of gable ends or pitch of the roof, ridge decorations or decorative cornices, and incorporate these into your sketch.

Where there is no easy solution as to where to build the new conservatory or how the design of the property would be compromised, it may be best to construct a simple glazed link from the main property to the new, keeping a distance between the two and allowing the new structure to stand alone visually. This option clearly takes up more space and does not have the advantage of insulating the wall of the house, but is well suited to pool houses where the size of extension might be out of proportion to the original building.

Many small urban houses can be extended into side entrances or alleyways running alongside a back room, creating informal dining areas or merely giving everyone a little more room. Extending the kitchen in this way can sometimes give the added space to put in an island unit, enabling the cook to look at a view rather than always facing a wall when cooking.

Where there is more space you should be able to consider building outwards into a garden to create a medium-sized or large conservatory. This opens up many more possibilities, since the space can be used for a wider range of functions. Although larger structures require a slightly bigger budget, the cost will not escalate in proportion with the size of the building; many of the costs remain the same whatever the size of the structure. You should remember, however, that the building time and disruption caused will last longer.

Even if there is no space at ground level, you may be able to build a conservatory at a higher level. This works particularly well above single-storey extensions, although you will need to check that the structure can be built upon. Ideally of course you should build both at once, and there is no point considering this until you have spoken to an expert. If you are able to create a high level sunroom, however, the views it will afford you will be well worth any hassle at the planning stages.

The message really is to ensure that you are clear what you want to achieve at the design stage. Proper prior preparation will enable the builder to plan and cost everything beforehand and reduce the chance of problems arising later.

ABOVE This modern urban conservatory is raised up above ground level, affording wonderful views over the city and, by being at tree canopy level, allowing a greater link with nature.

OPPOSITE A standard medium-sized conservatory can look very striking in a beautiful location such as this rural setting. This one is of sufficient size to allow both plants and people to inhabit the room comfortably.

CASE STUDY OF
a medium conservatory

Medium-sized conservatories fulfil a variety of functions, from garden rooms and chill-out zones to small offices and, as here, dining spaces. This example clearly shows how an added-on space can be used as a wonderful place to eat and relax.

BELOW By siting the conservatory at right angles to the house, the owners can access two separate parts of the garden and have views over a wide area on both sides of the structure.

The owners of this PVC-U conservatory have sited the new extension to the side of their single-storey house in the country, giving them light from two aspects and views of both the front and rear garden. A love of travel and an interest in oriental artefacts have influenced their choice of garden design and furnishings throughout the house, forming a cohesive link between house and garden.

The room is used year-round for dining. It has underfloor heating, backed up with an additional radiator, and forms part of the open plan kitchen in the original building. Large format creamy ceramic tiles, a good choice over underfloor heating, are also easy to clean, an important factor given the ample access to a sometimes muddy garden.

French doors from the conservatory open on to a paved terrace that is perfect for outdoor dining on one side, and the main part of the garden on the other. They have tip/tilt functions, meaning they can serve as a window when tilted inwards, or as sliding doors when set in the correct position, giving access to the rear sloping garden and providing a through draught on hot days. Two elegant light fittings shipped specially from a visit to Thailand provide a diffuse and restful light, and candles can be lit for romantic evenings.

The low windowsill around the conservatory provides a good place for carefully chosen plants and accessories with an oriental theme. This is carried through to the garden, with bamboo and grasses surrounding a Zen statue and a shishi odoshi (Japanese deer scarer), creating a contemplative and evergreen space.

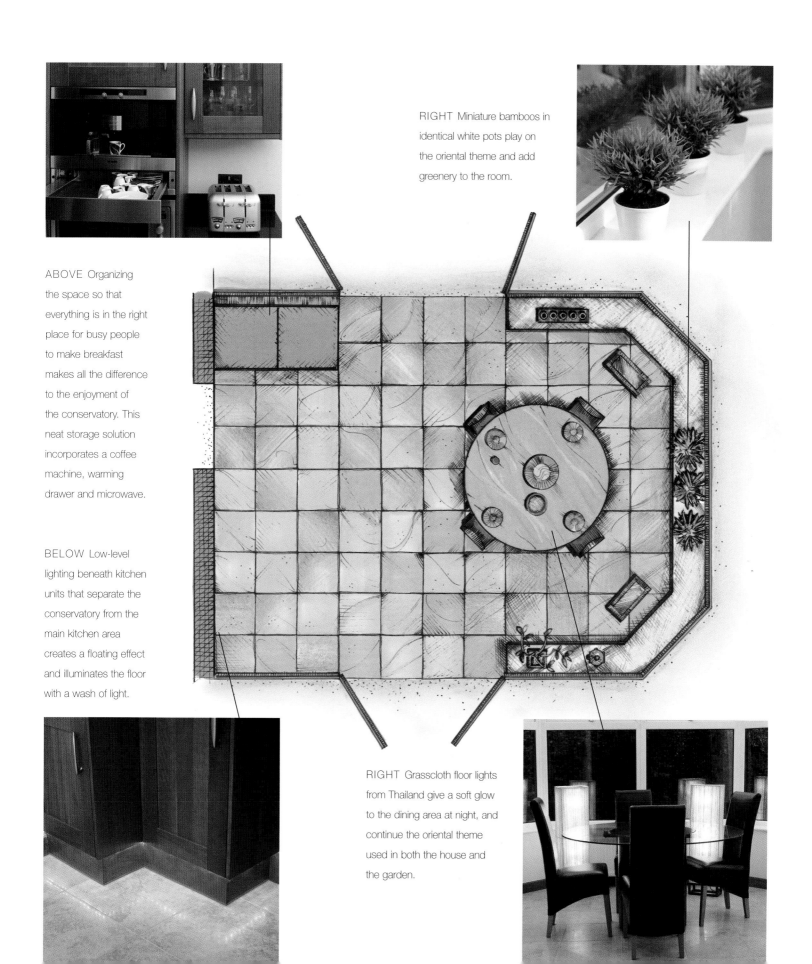

RIGHT Miniature bamboos in identical white pots play on the oriental theme and add greenery to the room.

ABOVE Organizing the space so that everything is in the right place for busy people to make breakfast makes all the difference to the enjoyment of the conservatory. This neat storage solution incorporates a coffee machine, warming drawer and microwave.

BELOW Low-level lighting beneath kitchen units that separate the conservatory from the main kitchen area creates a floating effect and illuminates the floor with a wash of light.

RIGHT Grasscloth floor lights from Thailand give a soft glow to the dining area at night, and continue the oriental theme used in both the house and the garden.

CASE STUDY OF
a large conservatory

A bold modern extension has transformed a rather dark and isolated kitchen into a dramatic and adaptable entertaining space that is both clutter-free and calm. Opening up the house to enjoy the view over the garden has made an older house work for 21st-century living.

BELOW Overhead light floods into the rear of the kitchen through a raised lantern light, and over the dining table through a frameless and almost flat sheet of glass. During the day there is a clear, uninterrupted view of the garden and at night a magical quality is achieved by well thought out lighting combined with the reflection of candles.

The main part of this typical semi-detached urban villa has a relatively traditional floor plan of cellular rooms linked by a rather dark corridor leading to the rear of the property. This has been dramatically extended to make a kitchen and dining room, creating a versatile space, especially for parties. The sense of being drenched with light, even on a winter's day, lifts the spirit, one of the unexpected delights of living under large expanses of glass.

Light over what could be a dark internal kitchen area is introduced by a raised lantern skylight with windows that open for good ventilation and that incorporates plaster uplights. A single sheet of laminated glass brings overhead light to the dining area, as well as large expanses of glass on two sides, with folding doors to the garden.

The owner has kept to a simple and elegant palette of off-white and neutral colours to unify the spaces, with finely jointed limestone flooring, polished concrete worktops

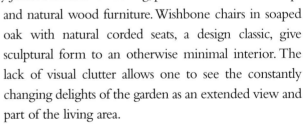

and natural wood furniture. Wishbone chairs in soaped oak with natural corded seats, a design classic, give sculptural form to an otherwise minimal interior. The lack of visual clutter allows one to see the constantly changing delights of the garden as an extended view and part of the living area.

Glass walls are recessed seamlessly into the floor, and silicone mastic where glass meets glass provides a minimal joint. Large panel glass doors concertina to either side of the opening giving an uninterrupted view to the outside area, and lock tightly and securely when closed at the turn of a handle.

Lighting has been carefully considered, with exterior uplights set into the stone surround echoing the downlights to the interior soffit, making the room quite magical at night, especially when candles and tea lights are included. This is an elegant and enhancing place to be, an effect achieved with clear ideas and a disciplined approach to keeping it that way.

LEFT The layout of the kitchen area allows the cook to admire the view or talk to guests while preparing meals.

RIGHT Citrus plants will thrive in a conservatory, adding scent and colour to an otherwise minimal room.

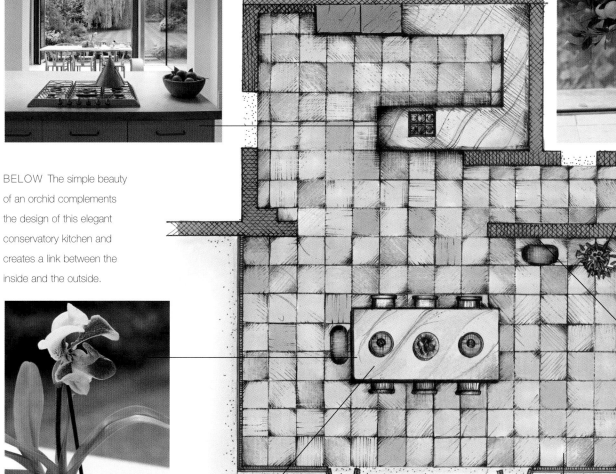

BELOW The simple beauty of an orchid complements the design of this elegant conservatory kitchen and creates a link between the inside and the outside.

BELOW Touchpad control plates allow different lighting scenes to be preset for different occasions.

LEFT Tea lights in a delightful collection of candle holders and coloured or plain tea light containers create a soft romantic glow at night and transform the space into a truly magical dining area.

RIGHT Crisp, clear lines and sharply defined angles in the construction are echoed by the precise shape of the small downlights, framing the sky above and intensifying the effect of the clouds.

CASE STUDY OF
an awkward space

When you have found the perfect location, but not quite the perfect layout of rooms, creative use of every available inch of space is the answer. Small spaces can be extremely efficient to work in if well planned, and are transformed by good natural light.

BELOW An unusual way of providing light to this kitchen was to glaze the roof with a single sheet of glass. The glass is strong enough to walk on for cleaning and is triple-glazed for preventing heat loss.

The owners of a listed (protected) building had found their dream house and garden, but the cellular layout of the rooms limited their use of the space. The existing kitchen proved too small for family living and provided inadequate heating. After careful consideration it was decided to utilize an outside space to the side of the house previously used as a storage area for garden equipment and bicycles. Despite being close to the boundary wall, permission was granted for a new kitchen that opened off the old one, as long as it was not visible from the street. This would provide a working kitchen linked to the family dining room as well as a desk for homework in one corner and full-height French doors opening on to the garden in summer.

The awkward site created problems, however, as in order to give enough wall space for cupboards, the design could only include one vertical window opening on to a side passage. In order to overcome this obstacle, the decision was taken to have a seamless sheet of glass for the roof, which would flood the whole kitchen with light and create a dramatic and unusual space. While appearing flat, the glass is on a five degree slope to enable rainwater to drain off and clean the glass. Triple-glazed for strength (a grown man can stand on it without it breaking) and to comply with building regulations, the ceiling is open to a view of the sky and the feeling of almost being outdoors gives what could have been an almost windowless room a wonderful sense of space and light.

Careful integration of a lighting track into the hollow section of the structural beams gives flexible lighting on surfaces, and spotlights at ground level cast a low-level glow on the floor. Motorized louvres and a concealed extractor fan at high level control heat build-up. Underfloor heating below the engineered oak floorboards frees up walls that might have been needed for conventional radiators for more useful purposes of storage and desking, and displaying art.

RIGHT Controls for lighting, heating and ventilation are neatly aligned in a handy yet unobtrusive location. A magnetic board, the width of the wall, provides a good place to store paperwork.

ABOVE Glass splashbacks around the sink are a practical wall finish and herbs thrive in the natural light from both the window and the overhead glass panel.

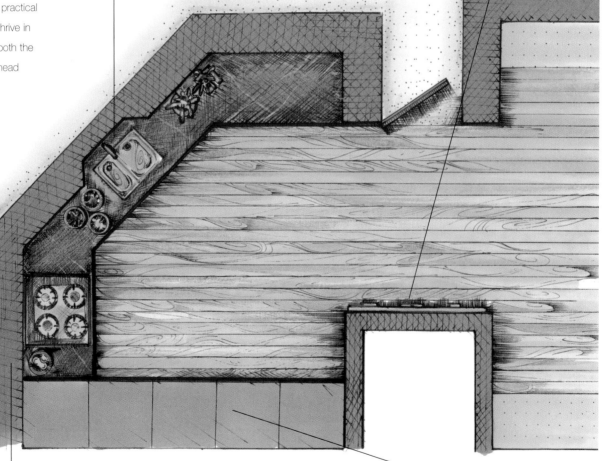

LEFT Adjustable wall-mounted track lighting gives focused light exactly where it is required. The lights can be manually angled as well as moved, giving the inhabitants great control over their positioning.

RIGHT All the storage space and most of the large kitchen appliances are meticulously organized behind a grid of simple yet stylish cupboard doors, creating a clutter-free kitchen workspace.

different styles

A quick look at the advertisements in interior and gardening magazines will reveal a huge number of manufacturers offering a wide variety of conservatories and sunrooms. Many off-the-peg ones are in traditional period styles, but there are usually other options, including pretty cottage-feel ones and cutting-edge modern designs.

Think carefully about the visual impact the new extension will have on your property. Having established that you can extend your space and that the size and shape will fulfil the function you intend for the room, look carefully at what others have done. Of course, much will depend on your budget, but seeking advice from specialist designers often saves making expensive mistakes in the long run. They will often come up with solutions you had not considered, and will point out any pitfalls at the outset.

Designs in the past grew out of the practical need to support heavy glass and hold it in place, and to provide heating, drainage and ventilation. Modern technology has provided many more options, however. These include creating a seamless box from special glazing held in place with silicon adhesive and structural columns made from glass. All of these factors mean that the period details are no longer necessary for practical purposes.

OPPOSITE This extension allows the building to be seen from outside, and provides a view to the garden from inside.

BELOW LEFT A modern seaside sunroom with a simple colour scheme looks inviting and delightful.

BELOW RIGHT Everything in this country conservatory has been chosen with care.

period conservatories

If you own a period building it is likely that a conservatory in a similar style will suit the structure best, although a clear glass structure can also work well on a period property, allowing the integrity of the building to be seen clearly. Conversely, period conservatories can look very odd on a relatively modern house, so you need to choose carefully.

BELOW The beauty of having a bespoke conservatory is that details can be faithfully copied and integrated into the new design. Here, the crenellations and finials have been carefully matched to the original building and the paint chosen to blend with the natural stone.

OPPOSITE A magnificent example of a Victorian conservatory with slim wrought iron columns and delicate beams. The Victorian passion for housing collections of newly discovered plants from around the world produced many such structures.

The most common period styles are derived from times in Britain when growing tender plants under glass was extremely popular. Georgian style from the mid-18th to the mid-19th century is typically plainer than later styles, and might be based on the design of some of the magnificent orangeries popular with the owners of grand houses and country estates. Solid roofs were common, with high windows opening down to floor level to enable plants to be wheeled out to the terrace in fine weather. When considering a conservatory in this style, look carefully at the glazing bars of your existing windows. In older houses built in the 18th and early 19th century these are often quite delicate sections with refined details. Matching these as closely as possible, and in the same paint colour, will help blend the new extension to the property visually.

Victorian conservatories conjure up images of serious plant collections, extravagantly ornate cast iron columns, ingenious systems for winding open ventilation flaps, and all sorts of heavy watering cans and gardening tools. Romantic and nostalgic, these structures were much prized by serious plantsmen during the Victorian period, when the needs of the plants they housed were often the prime consideration. In accordance with this, great attention was paid to installing proper shelving for displaying rare specimens in ideal conditions and ensuring there was sufficient room to store composts, tools, labels and fertilizers.

ABOVE The curved ogee aluminium roof gives height and good ventilation to a stairwell in this high-level conservatory – a sloping roof would not have such style. This design works as well with a traditional building as with a more modern one, and the choice of colours and formal planting add grandeur. Note the use of green marble tiles, which integrate with the greenery outside and enhance the inside/outside look perfectly.

Victorian style is usually characterized by a roof ridge at 90° to the property and a curved glazed bay to the front façade, although there are numerous interpretations of this and all the other styles. Roof lanterns at high level were often added to bring in extra light over extensions or add height and grandeur, and these can be used to great effect today to bring additional light and ventilation to a dark, stuffy room. Exuberant decorative motifs on the roof and woodwork were also popular, with deeply coloured stained glass used as details, often influenced by Gothic paintings and architecture of the time. Some new leaded glass designs can be rather crude so if stained glass is required today it might be better to keep to plain block colours. Alternative modern materials, such as aluminium, can also be used for the structure, making it lighter in weight and easier to maintain than original ones.

For the passionate modern gardener, this type of conservatory is a refuge, an oasis for therapeutic pottering as well as a place to sit back and enjoy the plants. A robust table can double up as both a work surface for potting up new specimens

or planting seeds, and a dining table, where the scent of jasmine or stephanotis can be enjoyed and the intricate beauty of the flowers admired.

Architectural salvage yards can often produce antique radiators or wrought iron furniture and ornaments, and provide old terracotta pots and tools to enhance the interior and create a sense of theatre. Even the odd spider is somehow more tolerable in a conservatory and acts as a biological control on other less welcome invaders. As with all things, there is a balance to be had – too many pieces of old junk (or spiders) are not desirable; it is how you make use of them that counts.

Standard Edwardian designs for the mass market are usually rather plainer than Victorian ones, with a simple gable end to a hipped roof. They are often square or rectangular in shape, but can retain some of the finials and other decorative elements associated with Victorian styles. This type can be a good option if you have a limited budget or want to keep things simple.

When adding a replica period conservatory to an old house it is important to relate the design to the angle of the existing roof and to use materials that will blend in sympathetically. Match the exterior walls of the property by using similar reclaimed bricks or stucco for the plinth (dwarf) wall, for example, and choosing flooring with a weathered appearance. Architectural salvage companies often have quantities of old stone or tile, which can look more interesting and authentic than new, depending on what look you want to achieve. Using the same flooring materials inside and out will help integrate the outside with the interior and soften the transition between both.

Manufacturers usually have a range of decorative roof crestings, finials, brackets and grilles to add finishing touches, and choosing appropriate door handles and window catches will all enhance the period design and add to the individuality of the end result, providing they are well made and detailed. Too many faux period details can detract from the simplicity of the structure and just look cheap.

LEFT Decorative crestings and finials can enhance the look of the period conservatory as long as they are of good quality and in keeping with the period of the house. Match them as closely as possible to existing detailing.

BELOW Crittall steel windows were popular in conservatories built in the early 20th century, but advances in double glazing and heat loss technology have made metal glazing bars a more efficient option.

cottage garden conservatories

The country cottage conjures up a romantic vision of life, but in reality these small houses are likely to have low ceilings, compact enclosed rooms and small windows. Adding a conservatory will help bring in some much-needed light, as well as providing an additional room with plenty of space for both humans and plants.

BELOW It is hard to resist the romantic charms of a thatched cottage in a country garden. A conservatory extension can provide a light-filled space, often lacking in these cottages, as well as a lush, calm indoor garden room.

The addition of a conservatory can often make a huge difference to a country cottage, adding extra space and a way of enjoying views of the countryside around and of observing nature in comfort. More informal designs somehow seem more suitable for this type of property, and this can be reflected in the style of garden, garden room and choice of plants. With more space outside in which to grow plants or create views across landscapes, the conservatory comes into its own as a place to start seeds off or to ripen the last of the summer's fruit and vegetables, or simply as a protected environment away from the local wildlife. Rural areas are

often several degrees colder than urban ones, and frosts more damaging, so the shelter provides an opportunity to grow tender plants for scent and colour under glass. The addition of a conservatory will also add an extra layer of insulation to the side of the cottage and help eliminate draughts.

Whatever form of construction you use, the new garden room should be in proportion to the overall size of the house, reflect the roof pitch, and blend in with the architectural style of the property without adding too much in the way of 'period' details unless they are bespoke and authentic replicas of existing mouldings or finials. The charm of the traditional cottage is that nothing is quite straight or machined, and any new conservatory is likely to be quite the opposite, with sharp angles and hard edges. Painting the framework of the new addition may help to minimize the impact – dark greens work particularly well if there are dense planting schemes or large trees to blend in with. The frameless all-glass structure is another option, allowing total clarity and not detracting from the vernacular design of the cottage. Just because one is in an old house doesn't mean one has to live with 18th- or 19th-century ideas.

The choice of planting can be whatever interests you or enhances the look of the conservatory. Country gardens can look pretty bleak in winter, so a few plants, which will give pleasure through the darker months, might be a good idea. Pelargoniums can often be kept going indoors long after the garden ones have succumbed to frost and there are colours to suit every taste. The scented varieties have pretty leaves which release aromas ranging from lemon to ginger and peppermint when bruised or brushed past. Stephanotis flowers during the winter and can be trained to climb and trail, softening the look of the structure with its evergreen leaves and smelling heavenly. Streptocarpus are both beautiful and obliging, managing to flower all year round, making them an essential. A few pots of herbs will enhance both the space and your cooking, and provide aroma and interest whatever the season.

Local auction sales can be rich hunting grounds for old Victorian terracotta pots and garden tools. The tools may not stand up to being used but can look interesting displayed on walls as a sort of bucolic installation art. The pots are beautiful in their own right, as well as being the best containers for plants, the rich patina having so much more character than the modern ones.

ABOVE Crisp white woodwork matches both the house paint as well as the profusion of Iceberg roses planted nearby. Simple dentil mouldings at the ridge and eaves add to the detailing and look just right in this small country conservatory. Lush planting around the base of the extension ensures a blurring of boundaries when viewed from both inside and out, making for a relaxing and scent-filled experience. Some evergreen plants would provide year-round colour and a good contrasting background for more colourful summer planting.

modern conservatories

Modern technology enables us to use glass in a way not previously possible and a 'period style' is no longer the only option. Layers of laminated glass that are strong enough to withstand attempts to break in can be used to transform dark spaces or to create the architectural ideal of the frameless glass box, while specialist finishes minimize heat loss and gain.

BELOW Glass fin columns and beams with silicone joints create the most seamless of systems for glazing. Triple-glazed, self-cleaning and with solar control coatings, this option is well worth considering for a modern design.

For many, the option of opening up the whole lower back wall of the living area by installing double-glazed folding or sliding doors transforms a space, making it an integral part of the property. Many older houses have single-storey kitchen extensions, and these can be adapted by inserting a glazed lantern or a single large sheet of laminated glass to form the top part of the flat roof. The addition of sliding or folding doors to the outside will complete the transformation. These sorts of alterations will need specialist advice from a structural engineer or architect, but will convert small cellular rooms into airy modern areas.

In many cities, where space is at a premium and the cost or impracticality of moving means that is not always an option, the answer is often to make the best use of basements. Older houses traditionally had basements with access to an outside area below the level of the garden, usually lacking light and often damp. Transformations have been achieved by extending outwards, digging out the part of the garden nearest to the property and installing a wall of glass doors. These open on to a newly paved terrace area suitable for alfresco dining or for children to play safely, overseen from within, and bring space and light to previously hard-to-use rooms. While not conservatories in the conventional sense, these alterations represent excellent new ways of living under glass and connecting to the outside world.

Garden rooms, porches or conservatories need not have the entire roof made of glass. Recent developments in 'living roofs' have made it possible to insulate a flat or gently sloping pitched roof with a mat of suitable plants, often stonecrop (*Sedum*). The structure consists of special drainage layers and a growing medium impregnated with plants, and can be installed over roofs that are specially constructed

BELOW Bold use of timber framing in a modern design creates an indoor garden and dining area.

BELOW RIGHT *Sedum* plants can be used insulate a flat or sloping roof.

RIGHT Glazing part of the roof to a single-storey extension and adding a door opening to the garden creates a modern, light space for dining. Well-chosen furniture and lighting makes this a comfortable, family-friendly space.

to take the added weight. This provides the advantages of good natural insulation against heat and cold leading to a reduction in energy costs as well as giving a green view from overlooking windows and providing a habitat for wildlife. Best installed and established before summer to prevent young plants being scorched by hot sun, these are now being included in many eco-housing schemes and need little attention once they have matured.

Stonecrops, of which there are many species for different conditions, thrive in nutrient-poor soil and will survive in all but the most arid desert conditions. They can change colour throughout the year depending on the species chosen, ranging from bright green in summer to a deep wine red in autumn, with the added bonus of frothy flowers in summer.

CASE STUDY OF

a modern conservatory

The rapid development of materials and technology in recent years and the ebb and flow of design trends can be seen in the range of modern conservatories on offer. This pioneering garden room is a case in point, since it pushed the boundaries of glass technology when it was first designed and won several architectural awards.

BELOW By enlarging window openings in the ground floor of this town house, a more flexible, open plan has been achieved between kitchen, dining and living areas. By excavating into the sloping site the impact of the extension on the outside is minimized.

This modern conservatory is a good example of how to adapt an early 19th-century house to accommodate the way we live in the 21st century. Using triple-laminated glass as structural beams and columns, clear silicone bonding and an invisible film of heating element applied to the laminated roof glass, this perfect glass box has transformed a Georgian house. The garden room links the kitchen and dining room and creates an open-plan living area, providing dining space and a comfortable place to read and listen to music, as well as enabling anyone in the kitchen to be part of the social interaction. Careful styling has eliminated any extraneous details that might detract from the purity of the extension.

Despite being in the city, this design allows one to be surrounded by lush greenery and bird life by day, and at night the structure is transformed by lighting concealed behind etched glass panels both at high and sill level, giving a soft glow of indirect light, the moon and the stars providing the ultimate backdrop.

On the shady side, the room does not overheat during the day, unlike some all-glass structures, and ventilation is easily controlled by opening a window or creating a through-draught by opening the door. The dwarf wall, which also has lighting set under etched glass panels, meets the garden seamlessly, the transition to the sloping ground filled with white stones where self-seeding ferns are beginning to grow.

LEFT A neat recessed downlight illuminates perfectly designed steps, which appear to be floating and are a stylish way of linking the level of the floor of the conservatory with the ground level outside. A pure white orchid on the sill of the wall adds a welcome floral note.

RIGHT Panes of triple-laminated glass are bonded with clear silicone to create a frameless modern box. An unobtrusive dwarf wall and pale wooden floors do not distract the eye, maintaining the purity of the uncluttered space and allowing the view of the garden outside to take centre stage.

ABOVE Every detail has been carefully considered – even the door handle has been made of glass.

RIGHT Extremely strong triple-glazed glass beams support the glass roof. Removable glass panels set against the wall of the house conceal discreet lighting.

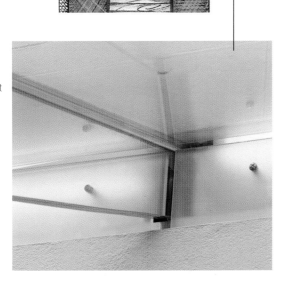

RIGHT This flexible space is sometimes used for informal family dining, when a table and chairs are brought in, but it works just as well as a relaxing space in which to curl up on an armchair and read, listen to music or simply enjoy the view after a day's work.

chapter four

practical factors

The choice of materials and construction will have a huge effect on the appearance of a conservatory, as will the colours chosen for the wall and floor finishes; the same building will look completely different in a dark colour compared to a pastel shade. Talk to experts about the relative merits of the constructions they offer and decide which one meets all your practical and aesthetic requirements. Short-term savings on cheap structures could mean long-term increases in heating or cooling costs and add less value to your home.

LEFT Classical columns and Roman-influenced chairs create a formal air in this stylish timber conservatory. Pale stone floors are both elegant and practical as they can be easily swept clean.

choosing materials

Having established the right design and position for the new conservatory extension, there are many other options to consider, from the materials used for the frame, the type of glass and the exterior details to flooring, heating, ventilation, power and lighting.

BELOW In this charming, airy conservatory the roof structure comprises a system that combines timber with metal. This strengthened material can be used in longer lengths than standard timber, but retains the appearance of wood. Solid timber window frames enhance the traditional feel of the room, while white paintwork and a light stone floor work well with simple yet elegant modern dining furniture.

Construction materials

Manufacturers tend to specialize in one or other of the most commonly used materials for framing the conservatory – PVC-U (unplasticized Poly Vinyl Chloride), aluminium, steel or timber – but may be able to offer all four. PVC-U is the least expensive of the materials that can be used and can be bought as a DIY option in many large home stores, but it can look rather plastic with less refined details. There are also environmental concerns, as it is difficult to recycle and its manufacture creates and releases one of the most toxic chemicals – dioxin. The most commonly used colour for this material is white, which can discolour and become scuffed over time. It is a good insulator, however, and can provide a very useful space at a relatively low cost.

Aluminium or galvanized steel frames provide a very good slim but strong profile and are a technically innovative way of constructing a conservatory. Many conservatory suppliers have different extrusions (some more complex than others) for holding different thicknesses of glass, providing internal draining bars and to aid assembly. It is worth talking to as many different suppliers as possible to discuss the merits of the system on offer. Curved roofs can also be constructed more easily from aluminium, combined with polycarbonate instead of glass. To reduce heat loss and condensation, the system should have thermal breaks and use stainless steel fastenings. Powder coating of the aluminium sections enables a wide range of colours to be chosen. If you do not like the look of the material, one option is for aluminium to be used for the roof sections and timber for the windows, giving the benefit of a strong roof and a good match with existing window frames.

Wood gives a solid traditional feel but, being a natural material, can be prone to movement if you do not use the highest-quality timber. Easy to work, it is ideal for replicating existing window details and mouldings, and also works well with double glazing. It will also complement other natural materials, such as stone, brick, slate and terracotta, used for

flooring or other areas. Maintenance is an issue with softwood timber, as without regular painting or sealing it can rot and decay. This is no more of a problem than with the timber window frames in many houses though, and regular maintenance of all aspects of your property is common sense. Well-seasoned hardwoods are ideal for the bespoke conservatory (being extremely durable and stable) and do not need to be painted – simply sealed regularly if that is the look you require. Whatever you use, it is important to ensure that the wood is from a renewable, sustainable source, and certified as such.

Frameless structures

Modern glass technology now enables frameless glass structures to be built, by bonding or laminating layers of glass together and by using glass fins as structural supports and beams. This option is most commonly used for one-off bespoke conservatories, including the ultimate 'glass box' that was for so long the holy grail of architects. These frameless designs look as good with historic or period buildings as with contemporary architecture and since the previous limitations on size and strength have been overcome there remain few limitations, other than cost. As the main raw material for making glass, silicon dioxide, is in plentiful supply and can be recycled, this is also a sustainable option.

Painted finishes

There is an almost unlimited palette of colours from specialist paint manufacturers if a painted finish is required. Pure white paint, although used on many of the original historic greenhouses, can look too pristine in some situations and there are some pretty soft olive greens and grey-blues that tend to work better with plants both inside and out. Many paint manufacturers now have beautiful ranges of coloured paints that enhance the appearance of the structure and help to blend the transition between the building and any planting.

ABOVE Powder-coated aluminium systems are easy to maintain and are very strong.

LEFT A detail of a laminated glass beam with a silicone mastic joint from a frameless conservatory. Most glass has a naturally green tint, which is more obvious with very thick glass and blends well with the green of the landscape.

flooring

When deciding what type of flooring to use, much depends on how you wish to use the new extension, what form of heating is used and what the floor finishes are leading to and from the conservatory. Ideally, the link between the inside and outside should be as seamless as possible, with similar or even identical materials on both sides of the divide.

Good preparation of the base for whatever material is chosen is the key to a trouble-free floor. For a new installation, it is vital that the concrete screed is perfectly level and is given time to dry out properly, which can take up to six weeks depending on what time of year the work is carried out. As this is a large and expensive area of your conservatory it is worth looking at all the options and taking specialist advice.

Flooring, as one of the largest areas of solid material, will play a major role in how the finished room will look. As a general rule of thumb, the lighter the colour, the bigger the room will appear. Traditional period conservatories, designed primarily for plants, had floors that were practical enough to withstand spilt water, soil and grit, and were often made of brick or quarry tiles in black and red. These are still good choices for a country property, but for many who now use the conservatory extension simply as an extra living space, pale limestones or ceramic tiles are often chosen as they provide a neutral background and are good conductors of underfloor heating.

If the thought of just hard floors does not appeal, woven rugs made from natural fibres such as grass, coir and sisal add texture and colour and have the right indoor/outdoor feel.

Tiles, stone, brick

The practical finishes for conservatory flooring are those that are easily cleaned, not harmed by condensation or by being exposed to strong light and which are able to withstand mud and grit brought in from outside. Ceramic tiles are now available in very

large sizes and in a variety of textures, including many that look remarkably like stone or slate, without being porous. These are a practical, affordable choice and are easy to maintain, usually by washing with a damp mop. They are not, however, usually suitable for outdoor situations unless specifically stated. Quarry tiles are unglazed and very durable, can be used both inside and out and come in some muted earth colours, making them suitable for traditional country conservatories.

Natural stone is an obvious choice for the indoor/outdoor look and works well over underfloor heating. It can have a variety of surface textures according to the way it is cut and finished – finishes range from honed to flamed and riven – and they can make a big difference to the appearance as well as the danger of slipping. Stone or slate can also be used for windowsills to match the floor – there are some beautiful green slates, which blend in well with a green landscape, and a rich grey-black which looks very architectural and crisp. Take advice from a reputable supplier as some stones are harder than others depending on where they were

ABOVE Original Victorian tiles are hard wearing and look right in old conservatories. Here a mixture of quarry tiles form a delightful geometric pattern edged by an ornate iron grille.

OPPOSITE Large format tiles create a clean, contemporary finish and conduct heat well over underfloor heating. Here a bold graphic patterned rug adds accent colour and softness to the room.

BELOW Stone is the predominant feature in this conservatory, from the floor and walls to the fire surround and the colour of the paint. Heating grilles provide a strong border feature.

sourced, and not all are suitable for outside use in very cold areas. Once sealed, stone is easily maintained by sweeping and damp mopping, but can still absorb stains such as red wine or acids. If the area is heavily trafficked it will be essential to have the stone professionally cleaned and resealed from time to time.

An alternative to natural stone is reconstituted stone. Sometimes known as technical stone, it is produced by combining high-grade marble chippings with specially formulated polyester resins and colour pigments. These are available in large-format tiles in a good variety of stone colours and can give a very smart contemporary finish at a more affordable cost than natural stone, with none of the maintenance problems of the real thing.

For a conservatory where there will be a lot of plants, brick can be a beautiful, rustic flooring material, especially when it is laid in a herringbone pattern. You should be aware, however, that it can be slippery. Salvage companies can be useful sources of reclaimed bricks, especially old handmade ones, which have a lovely texture and look particularly good in a country cottage or barn conversion. It is good practice when buying salvaged materials to order about 10 per cent more than is needed, in case of breakages or for future use.

Wood

Timber flooring is not usually a good choice in rooms where there is high humidity or water is likely to be spilled. If, however, the conservatory is mainly used as a living room, this is a suitable material. Many suppliers now offer engineered timber boards, a 'sandwich' of hardwood stabilized with a core and base with finishes suitable for areas such as kitchens and bathrooms. These engineered boards are generally the only choice of wood flooring that is compatible with underfloor heating. They are considerably more expensive than simple timber floors but are more stable in varying temperatures, although dark colours may fade under strong light. If there is direct access from the garden or where mud and grit might be brought in, it is a good idea to design in a mat well, since grit on shoes could damage the wood.

Although not technically a wood, bamboo is often recommended for areas of high humidity and gives the same warm appearance as wood. As bamboo is a sustainable product, fast growing and mature at three years' growth, this is an ecologically sound choice.

Modern alternatives

Contemporary designers like the slightly industrial appearance of polished concrete, a highly practical finish if laid correctly. This produces a smooth, seamless floor polished to a finish ranging from satin to high gloss. The skill and experience of the installer, as ever, is paramount, and new concrete will need to 'cure' for 4–6 weeks before being polished. Concrete can crack, however, if there is any movement in the floor, as can happen in most houses, and one may have to accept this as part of the industrial look.

In the same category, poured resin floors are now being used in contemporary interiors. Once mainly used in factories, warehouses and institutional buildings, this is a seamless, hygienic material and is available in a wide range of colours. For a similar appearance, rubber tiles can used. This is not a conventional look, but it is perfect if you want vibrant colours and a practical finish around swimming pools or children's play areas. Rubber stud tiles come in clear, bright colours, make a good non-slip surface and would give a high-tech look to a modern glass extension. These last three finishes all need to be installed by specialists, and may not be found in the local flooring company.

ABOVE RIGHT A timber floor looks right with the pastel-coloured wooden units in this light-filled conservatory kitchen. Ensure that the floor you have chosen is suitable for use in areas with heavy traffic and that may get wet.

RIGHT A stone floor is one of the most practical and pleasing if the budget allows. Perfect over underfloor heating, it can also be used outside if the correct stone is specified, creating a link between the two areas.

glass

Whatever structural material is used for the framework, the common and most defining element in a conservatory is glass. There are various types available, from single-, double- and triple-glazed materials and super-strong safety glass to innovative varieties that help prevent heat loss or gain and even self-cleaning glass.

BELOW Triple-glazed glass beams bonded to glass eliminate the need for a frame in this seamless glass box. Etched glass panels conceal lighting from underneath.

The development of double glazing, two sheets of glass separated by dehumidified air or sometimes with a gas such as argon, and factory sealed with metal strips around the edges, revolutionized conservatory construction and made it possible to use them year round, keeping warmth in and sound out. Today, there is a wide variety of highly technical glass, from nanogel particles and photovoltaic cells to tinted, laminated and self-cleaning glass. Toughened or laminated glass, which either crazes or, if completely broken, forms 'dice' shaped pieces that do much less harm, should be used in overhead situations where shards of conventional broken glass could be lethal. Some of these are currently very expensive and are used for commercial buildings but, as with many technological advances, may become more affordable with time.

Solar control

For most conservatory glazing, the issues will be to do with heat gain in sunny situations or in hot countries, and with heat loss in cold climates. Glass is available coated with microscopic particles to control heat loss or gain. Conserving the heat gained from the sun is an important factor in cooler climates and is the subject of much regulation with regards to reducing the amount of fuel used in the home. To conserve the heat gained, the use of Low E (Low Emissivity) glass is now standard and often required by regulation. Low E glass is coated with virtually invisible, metal or metallic oxide layers used on the inner pane of glass to avoid heat loss. The Low E coating reduces the infrared radiation from a warm pane of glass to a cooler pane, thereby lowering the U-factor of the window and reducing the CO_2 emissions associated with heating.

When the metallic oxide coating is used on the outer pane it can reflect up to 75 per cent of the solar energy back into the atmosphere to avoid heat gain. Major glass manufacturers, such as Pilkington and St Gobain Glass, have excellent and informative websites that explain the many and varied products that are suitable for each particular situation. Other glass is available tinted to reduce heat transmission or as a laminate, where the inner layer of the sandwich is tinted, giving good insulation properties.

A reputable conservatory manufacturer or designer will be able to guide you on the use of specialist glazing, how to comply with local regulation, and what the costs of each option are.

Safety glass

Where glass is used overhead, at low level or in and around doors, windows and screens, standards need to be met to protect against accidental human impact, such as children running into a patio door. The location of the glass and its size determines the classification of impact resistance that should be used. There are three types of common safety glass:

• Toughened glass is up to five times stronger than ordinary glass and it breaks into small, safe granular pieces when smashed.

• Laminated glass consists of two pieces of glass bonded together with a clear plastic interlayer so it cracks when broken but stays in position, reducing the risk of injury.

• Wired safety glass has metal mesh embedded within the glass and it behaves like laminated glass when it is broken.

ABOVE RIGHT Laminated glass is very strong and can be used for small or vast structures, such as the roof of the Great Glasshouse at the National Botanic Garden of Wales.

RIGHT Where large expanses of glazing are used, tinted glass can reduce heat transmission and uncomfortable glare, making it easier to control both light and temperature levels.

ventilation

Using glass can lead to trapped heat and heavy condensation – not good for most plants or furnishings. Many plant diseases are partly caused by poor ventilation and lack of circulating air, and there is little that is more off-putting than sitting in a space surrounded by mould and mildew. Good ventilation is therefore very important, and there are several options available.

LEFT The traditional lantern design allows more light to flood in through the vertical element as well as the pitched roof lights. Ventilation can be achieved by opening the small windows. Here, uplighters will give a gentle glow of light at night. These will attract insects, which will fry themselves on the lamps, so make sure the light fitting can be reached safely for cleaning!

BELOW High level louvres give the option of passive natural ventilation or mechanical extraction when necessary.

The simplest way of ventilating any room is to open doors and windows to create a through-draught, but this requires you to be present at all times. Leaving doors and windows open unattended is not a safe option, but sash bolts and movement sensor alarms should be added as an essential part of the design to enable windows to be left slightly open.

Since hot air rises, the most practical place for ventilation is in the roof structure and the traditional lantern design used in many conservatories is ideal for this, trapping hot air at its highest point and allowing vertical louvres or openings to be incorporated into the sides. Alternatively, conservatories with a pitched roof and a ridge structure may have ventilators built in quite unobtrusively, operated manually with motors or a custom-made long pole, which will need to be kept in a suitable place.

Louvres can be motorized and controlled by a switch, and left in the open position when you go away, making them a good choice. Alternatively, an extractor fan can be built into the structure and regulated by switch or operated thermostatically.

Overhead ceiling fans do little for true ventilation, but do stir the air up and create a cooling effect on the skin, mixing the cooler air at low level with the hot air above and creating movement. They can be noisy, however, and need a reasonable ceiling height to avoid scalping tall visitors.

Electronically operated trickle vents can be incorporated into the roof ridge of some designs, but more muscular ventilation will be needed during

RIGHT This studio is on the shady side of the house, providing the perfect quality of light for an artist, but being at the top of the building can still become quickly overheated without good ventilation. Opening windows to create a through-draught is the easiest solution to this problem when someone is at home.

BELOW RIGHT Simple brass winding systems operated manually by a long pole enable high-level windows to be opened easily. Open windows at high level are less likely to be accessible to burglars or visiting cats, so are safer than other windows, but you should never leave a window open unattended. The light will attract insects, so you may need to consider some form of insect repellent or screening.

very hot weather, especially in sunny situations. Solar powered vents, which are fitted into the roof and open and close automatically depending on the temperature, are also now available and provide a relatively inexpensive and 'green' option.

Insect control

With ventilation openings come insects. These will be attracted to light and any plants, and inevitably end up at high level where they are difficult to reach. Where this is a significant problem, fly screens can be included in the design, or simple chain curtains hung at doorways. Citronella candles may help to keep some insects away. Plug-in devices that vaporize tablets of a granular form of a pyrethroid agent, Transfluthrin, have been popular in southern Europe for some years, and do seem to be effective. Fly papers and insectocuters may be efficient but do little to add to the charm of the space.

heating

Despite the arrival of special types of heat-efficient glass, conservatories, like any room, can become cold during the winter. This is not only off-putting if you want to relax in the space, but it can also be damaging for the tender plants often grown there. Some form of heating is, therefore, essential in cold and temperate climates.

ABOVE Keeping the temperature at a comfortable level for people and plants is an important factor in the design of conservatories and needs to be carefully considered at the outset.

OPPOSITE The specialist conservatory blinds used in this sophisticated scheme reduce glare and heat gain, while heating is recessed into the floor beneath unobtrusive, decorative grilles, bringing warmth to all corners.

Underfloor heating is currently one of the best ways of heating areas where conventional radiators could be either unsightly or difficult to site, such as kitchens, bathrooms and conservatories. This heating mechanism works best under stone or tile floors and is especially good at evenly distributing heat over the entire area. This means that the system can be run at a lower temperature than radiators, using less energy and reducing fuel bills.

Many conservatory makers recommend the use of hot pipes set in floor trenches and covered with a decorative grille. This option works well with period conservatories, since the metal covering grille gives the effect of a border around the room as part of the overall interior design as well as leaving the walls free of radiators. Look carefully at all the options before you make the final decision.

There are some very attractive clear glass radiators available, ranging from integrated systems to simple plug-in heaters. These discreet alternatives are splash resistant, but would not be suitable for a conservatory designed mainly for plants, where large amounts of water are used and where waterproof sockets and fittings will be needed.

Geothermal energy

If major work is needed in the garden when the conservatory is being built, installation of ground pumps might be worth considering if you have plenty of land available. These pumps transfer the earth's heat from below the ground by way of coils laid into deep trenches or boreholes. Where outside space is limited, a compressor system in the property may be required. A qualified heating engineer will be able to advise on the feasibility of these possibilities.

Use of geothermal energy is currently not cost-effective as the initial outlay is expensive, although price rises in other fuels may soon mean that the initial cost is worth bearing, but it does reduce the carbon footprint considerably. It is certainly worth investigating whether government grants are available, or whether your current utility supplier offers any cashback deals. In some countries, home owners are now required to declare the energy efficiency of their property when selling it, so any steps taken to reduce carbon emissions could be a positive factor in the sale. However the room is heated, there should be a thermostat to control the temperature at all times.

power

Unless a conservatory is going to be used solely for plants, you are likely to require power outlets. The number and position of these will depend on what the room is going to be used for – offices and living rooms will require more outlets than, say, a dining room, and a telephone outlet or television aerial socket may also be needed.

Make sure all the utilities are in the right place at the start of the project. It is better to have too many sockets than too few, and as you may well spend a lot of time in this versatile space it is better to have all the creature comforts to hand. Careful planning of furniture layouts will ensure that such necessities as hard-wired telephone points are in the right place – it can be both unsightly and dangerous to have cables stretching around a space, due to sockets being in the wrong place.

It is worth taking the time to consider how best to disguise or conceal sockets and wires. Fitted shelving units with space for a sound system and speakers are a good option, as they fulfil several functions at once and can look attractive. These should be positioned against a solid wall and may need to be specially made to fit the space, especially if there is a sloping roof.

Lighting controls are very important, and should be positioned where they will be most convenient. You may require different circuits to create subtle moods, and need to decide early on whether you want any free-standing light sources, which will require a power outlet.

Blinds and ventilation mechanisms may need to be remotely operated if they are at high level. If these are electronically controlled they will need wiring brought to the correct positions at an early stage in the building process, which is why good planning at the outset is so important. It always costs considerably more to add later, and the design will be compromised.

OPPOSITE Careful thought has gone into storage, audio-visual installation and reducing the amount of clutter in this dining space. Fitted shelving units not only conceal unsightly wires but also keep the space looking tidy.

BELOW Plan where sockets and light switches will be needed and put in more than you need. Great care should be taken when watering plants near power outlets and you should not position them too close together.

lighting

The whole point of conservatory rooms is that they are filled with natural light and allow us to connect with the landscape, whether it is in town or country. During daylight hours, natural overhead light is usually more than enough, even on dull days, but it is at night when the real drama can be heightened by creative use of artificial lighting.

ABOVE An elaborate, ornate chandelier sets the scene for a special event. Always check that the structure can take the weight of the light fitting.

OPPOSITE Lights set into the exterior soffit and the edge of the steps cast a magical glow on this stunning conservatory. Candles and tea lights on the table give a soft romantic feel and provide a decorative touch to a deceptively simple scheme.

Lighting is one of the fastest growing technologies, with new advances becoming more affordable and available to everyone prepared to do a little homework. Good lighting can transform a room, enhancing the good parts and playing down the less good, and dramatizing an artwork or architectural feature by directing the eye. Rather than flooding the whole room with an even, flat light, think how much more interesting to have light just where you need it, with softer areas where you do not; highlighting beautiful things and lowlighting those that are perhaps better not viewed too critically.

A wealth of choice

One of the most important factors in creating the right interior is in the design of the lighting. Conservatories pose a particular problem, usually having too much light during daylight hours and insufficient lighting at night. Much will depend on the construction of the roof and whether it is solid or made of glass, and of course, the way the room is used. With a solid roof it is easy to install downlights or to hang pendant or lantern lights combined with some floor-mounted uplights to create a soft, flattering light. With a glass roof the problem is more complex and requires careful thought at the planning stage. With a conventional ridge structure, wiring can be taken through the box section and lighting brought to the appropriate points. Simple chandeliers can be effective in the right setting, adding sparkle in the reflective glass and an air of frivolity in an otherwise linear space, and there are many inexpensive modern interpretations of the chandelier which can work very well and provide an interesting centrepiece.

Wall-mounted lights can provide both uplight and downlight, and are useful where the extension is built on to the outside wall of an existing house and there is sufficient wall space to accommodate them. These provide good ambient light

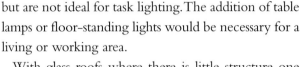

but are not ideal for task lighting. The addition of table lamps or floor-standing lights would be necessary for a living or working area.

With glass roofs where there is little structure one possibility is to use low voltage bare wire lighting. This consists of two low voltage (12v) cables tensioned from side to side of the area to be lit, carrying fittings that can be suspended, and directed to light seating areas or work tops or to illuminate sculpture or plants. Track-mounted spotlights, where the track is incorporated into the framework of the structure or suspended from the ceiling, can be a useful way of providing light at different angles. These spotlights can be directed to illuminate areas as needed and, with low voltage tracks and fittings, are small enough not to be intrusive. By reflecting the light off walls, glare can be avoided, and the linear track enables fittings to be placed anywhere along the length of the track, which is useful if you change the position of furniture in the room.

Other options

With the need to conserve energy becoming ever more important, the use of more technically advanced lighting should be considered. Cold cathode lighting strips can be used, set behind cove mouldings or around the perimeter of dropped ceilings, providing a long life and low heat output. LED (Light Emitting Diodes) lighting is the ultimate in long-life, low-heat lighting and can even be embedded invisibly into glass, giving the effect of tiny twinkling stars. LED light fittings can be used at skirting (base) board level to illuminate the floor – a surprisingly pleasing and practical effect – or set into the ground outside to light paths and walkways. The LEDs can be used to brighten stairs and steps very effectively, set into the skirtings or side wall of each stair tread, but must be suitable for external usage.

TOP Painted plaster uplights bounce light off the glass of lantern structures, creating a relaxing atmosphere at night.

ABOVE Inexpensive low-voltage lighting in a skirting (base) board gives a surprisingly good light and works especially well in smaller conservatories.

Creating an atmosphere

For the more sophisticated installation, lights can be set on different circuits to create different moods either by manual switching or by preset electronic systems. Scenes can be set from super-bright to seriously seductive or just soft, soothing scenarios. Remember that if the lighting is too bright it will reflect on large areas of glass, not only dazzling to the eye, but lessening the effect of any garden or terrace lighting. This is an option that needs specialist advice from a lighting designer, which may be expensive, but it is one of the best investments one can make.

Where there are plants and well-chosen planters and pots, these can be subtly lit to outline their shape and texture to dramatic effect. A recessed floor light illuminating a simple yet stylish pot can transform it into an object of beauty at night, outlining its curves and patina, and showing the intricate traceries of the plant's foliage.

Outdoor lighting

External lighting should not be intrusive to neighbours, but subtle, showing the organic beauty of a tree or uplighting a column or architectural feature to its full dramatic effect. Think of the way sunlight highlights some features, casting others into shade and creating a harmonious picture. Water features come into their own at night, with lighting bringing an extra dimension to the sparkling water, whether it is a simple bubbling spout or a larger pool or fountain. The garden can become a magical place even in the depths of winter, and summer evenings enhanced by enjoying the delicate tracery of foliage and flowers.

Candles, flares and tea lights can create a flickering drama on a summer's evening, but care must be taken where there are small children, and candles should never be left unattended. Paths and steps are made safer by low-level lighting to wash a walkway with gentle light and make a seamless transition from indoors to out. It is always important to take professional advice when installing any outdoor lighting.

BELOW LEFT Tea lights in pretty perforated containers can be used to mark paths and steps leading up to a garden room for a party or a summer barbecue. Great care should always be taken if you are using candles when children are around.

BELOW There is a huge number of outdoor lanterns available in a range of styles, from sleek modern lights to more romantic Moroccan-style affairs, such as this outdoor lamp. Most need to be suspended, either from a porch or veranda or on a free-standing bird feeder pole with an S-shaped hook.

chapter five

decorative features

Apart from being places for growing plants, conservatories have no particular traditions for their interior design. The key thing is practicality; if the conservatory is connected to a garden, which will inevitably result in some dirt being brought in, then the decorative features need to be able to withstand a bit of wear and tear. They also need to be resistant to bright light and some humidity. If the room contains plants, it may be best to stick to natural or horticultural items, such as collections of stones or shells, straw gardening hats or attractive watering cans.

LEFT A conservatory is a place to indulge in a little theatre. Here, a collection of antique furniture looks good in a contemporary setting and is complemented by the choice of plants.

finishing touches

There is a huge range of furniture, blinds and soft furnishings suitable for conservatories available, and which you choose will depend on the size and colour scheme of the rest of the room, your budget, and personal preference.

OPPOSITE Sculptural plants and a black and white colour scheme make a strong statement in this conservatory.

BELOW Restrained simplicity bathed in glorious light needs no added decoration.

The best conservatories are generally those treated simply, with pale paintwork and natural materials to enhance the feeling of light, airiness and a sense of outdoor living. For some, the sheer beauty of living in a pure, glazed room with a spectacular panorama will need no applied decoration, but will rely on the carefully chosen fittings, detailing and flooring materials to provide visual pleasure. For others the desire to introduce appropriately themed fabrics, furniture and accessories to personalize the room is irresistible. Whatever your preference, the conservatory should above all be where you can relax, put your feet up and look out at the world.

There are no specific traditions attached to these spaces when used as living rooms, so they provide a great opportunity to have some fun and try out a different style. You do not need to spend a fortune either: single, bold, sculptural objects such as an oversized plant pot or urn can look wonderful against glass, contrasting with plant foliage and leading your eye outwards, while collections of attractive old gardening tools can look like works of art if they are sensitively grouped together on a wall, and these are often to be found cheaply at house sales and secondhand shops.

The late designer David Hicks painted large but inexpensive plastic flower pots black to great effect, proving that good interiors do not have to be expensive, just inventive and disciplined.

colour schemes

The overall design of the conservatory or sunroom extension will influence how the interior is treated, from pure urban minimalism to a traditional country garden style, but where the extension is very clearly a garden room it can be a chance to play with materials and accessories that relate to the horticultural origins of the space.

BELOW White always looks fresh. Here, a blue and white jug (pitcher) of flowers and a red flowering plant provide the only colour necessary.

OPPOSITE A palette of warm terracotta, dark wood and faded turquoise colours lends this large conservatory a homely Mediterranean air.

As sunlight fades everything out in a conservatory, it seems sensible to choose bleached-out colours to start with, since they add a feeling of informality to a scheme and go well with the indoor/outdoor theme. Much depends on geographic location, but generally soft grey-greens and blues go well with gardens and plants, white goes with everything and natural stone colours often provide the best background for displaying plants or decorative items. The colours and materials of the areas around the outside must also be considered, so it is important to stand back and look critically at all the elements, tones and textures that exist, and work with them for a harmonious effect.

A subdued colour scheme will feel comfortable and relaxing, and can be enlivened by small amounts of colour from flowering plants or cushions and rugs. Keeping to a neutral palette of colours will allow the view and the sky to dominate or heighten the importance of well-chosen artefacts.

Using single colours can unite a space and provide a good backdrop to bolder and more idiosyncratic pieces. It is useful to assemble samples of all the finishes together and view them at different times of day, from very bright sunlight to artificial light at night. Paint colours, particularly subtle shades, can be notoriously difficult to choose, and are best seen painted from a sample pot on to a large surface rather than just being viewed on printed shade cards. Keep all the chosen samples together in a box and take them with you when you go shopping for fabrics and other accessories to ensure you get something that is going to harmonize with the colour scheme.

choosing furniture

Furniture made from cane, rattan and wicker has the right indoor/outdoor feel, being lightweight and airy and made of natural materials. Cast iron, much loved by the Victorians, is cold and unyielding to sit on and is also extremely heavy. As pleasurable relaxation is part of the appeal of conservatories it seems worth choosing comfort over an outdated style.

Many classic modern furniture pieces work very well in a conservatory or sunroom. They often have sculptural shapes, some have cheerful colours to enliven neutral spaces, and they are usually lightweight, informal and spare enough not to block views. Natural wood is also a good choice as, combined with a simple linen cushion, it can look even better when bleached and aged by sunlight.

Many manufacturers of outdoor furniture are now producing such stylish and technically innovative designs they are almost too good to leave outdoors, and would look particularly striking in a conservatory. It will be made to withstand the elements, including ultraviolet light, so will be perfect for use under glass too. Woven chairs made of a coaxial structure of stretch-resistant coated polyester fibre look like natural cane, but are softer and longer-lasting and can be taken outside. As this material does not absorb moisture it is especially suitable for humid areas, and of course is very simple to

LEFT A classic Eames lounge chair and footstool make the perfect place to read quietly or simply admire the garden beyond. Nothing obscures the view.

RIGHT A wonderfully theatrical arrangement of interesting shapes and textures have been grouped together to form an eclectic corner in this garden room.

clean, making it perfect where small children (or messy adults) are around. High-tech yarns, which can be dyed to beautiful colours, have the texture of soft rope and are water- and UV-proof, look equally good indoors or out and are used to create furniture with very contemporary designs. There are even outdoor rugs that will withstand any amount of wet and muddy feet tramping in from the garden and still look like an expensive woven carpet.

Because conservatories are all about light, it makes sense to choose simple, light furniture that doesn't obstruct or compete with the view. An assortment of wooden chairs can be transformed by painting or spraying them all the same matt (flat) colour – white or pale pastels work well and look fresh. Cushions with washable covers can add colour and softness.

Conservatories are wonderful for relaxing in and chairs with footstools are perfect for an indulgent reading session or well-earned rest. Combined with down-filled cushions and a cashmere throw, they can turn a simple space into a scene of ultimate luxury.

ABOVE Classic modern designer chairs have been chosen to add colour to a crisp, uncluttered contemporary conservatory. These chairs are robust, easy to clean and will not fade under the strong light from overhead glazing, making them the perfect choice for a family dining room which becomes one with the garden on fine days. The pastel shades work well with the view of the garden beyond.

choosing fabric

Any upholstery in a conservatory should ideally be made from materials that will not fade or rot. Several manufacturers have wonderful ranges of indoor/outdoor fabrics that look and feel like expensive and delicate yarns, but which are in fact solution-dyed acrylics that can be left outside in all weathers, by swimming pools, or even be scrubbed with bleach!

RIGHT Organic fabrics, such as hemp, bamboo and cotton, in natural colours made without the use of chemicals are becoming more popular.

BELOW This bold, exuberant scheme combines the vivid colours of summer flowers in graphic prints.

If you prefer to use natural materials, such as linen, hemp, bamboo and cotton, choose tough fabrics in light, neutral colours that will still look good as they fade. Silk is not recommended, since strong light will rot the fabric and fade jewel colours, although there are some more robust undyed silks that will be fine in shaded corners.

Generally where the room leads out to a garden it is sensible to choose fabrics that are hard-wearing and can be cleaned easily. There may be times when

chairs and tables are taken into the garden, so weatherproof finishes that will blend in with the surroundings are a good choice. Simple and sparing patterns generally work better than large strident designs, although these can be used to great effect as cushions, and particularly if the design has relevance to nature, such as a graphic leaf or the outline of a tree or skeletal seedhead. The beauty of the natural world is not always in bright colours but often in subtle textures and tones, and this is one way of approaching the interior design of the garden room. Even seemingly eclectic designs where colour and pattern run riot are often carefully put together by designers, with a common theme uniting them.

As the seasons change, so too can the furnishings. One famous architect changes the colour of the cushions in his otherwise white home environment according to the time of year: red for winter, blue for spring, green for summer and yellow for autumn.

Careful thought should be given to what textures work well in combination. Suede and linen for cushions look natural and go well together, and interest can be introduced with corded trims or large horn or mother-of-pearl buttons. If real suede is too delicate there are faux suedes that can be put in the washing machine, which come in the most beautiful colours and feel suitably luxurious. In the colder months, wool or cashmere throws add indulgent luxury as well as colour and texture, and inexpensive rugs can feel warmer underfoot when the outlook is chilly.

TOP RIGHT Cushions can provide a splash of colour and tie in with the plant theme of a garden room. This one looks especially striking against the white upholstery of the simple chair, and enhances the hothouse feel of the bright plants in the background.

RIGHT A simple linen-covered armchair, faux fur cushions and a neutral cashmere throw make this sunroom an indulgent place in which to relax and unwind. Elegant scented flowers add to the experience, as do a good book and a glass of something chilled.

choosing accessories

Having completed all the other cosmetic features of the conservatory, it is important that you maintain concentration when choosing the finishing touches such as plant pots, sculpture or artworks, or all your hard work could be marred by an ill-chosen piece. It is often best to leave these decisions until you have finished the rest of the decoration so you can see what is required.

ABOVE One sculptural planter, such as this magnificent ceramic pot, can be much more dramatic than a lot of mismatched small pots.

RIGHT Terracotta pots are the best choice for plants, as they allow water to drain away, but they do leave damp marks. One solution is to arrange the pots in another container, such as this Wardian case.

With the selection of accessories for the home growing bigger year by year, one needs to exercise a bit of discipline to prevent the conservatory from looking cluttered. We often acquire an assortment of vases, pictures, ornaments and plants from friends and relatives and the temptation is to put them all in the same room and hope for the best. This often results in the conservatory looking very different from the elegant and calm space shown in magazines and catalogues.

Planters, pots and containers

There are many different shapes, sizes, colours and materials when it comes to plant containers, and what you use will depend on the type of surface the pot will be positioned on and the size of the plant. Whatever you choose, it is important that you make sure that any excess water can drain away from the plant, and that large pots can be moved easily from time to time to allow you to clean properly.

Terracotta pots have been the most popular choice for many years for direct planting due to their porous qualities, although this does mean that they make damp marks on wooden floors and their matching saucers will do the same unless they have been sealed in some way. Most plants prefer to dry out between waterings and terracotta allows moisture to be taken away from the roots. Collections of old terracotta pots look good and can occasionally be found in auction sales, with a wonderful aged patina and in usefully differing sizes. They are especially suited to country conservatories or where you want a rustic look, but for a contemporary urban conservatory living area, you may want something different.

Uniformity of colour or shape often makes for a more considered look, especially when pots are grouped together. Groups of dissimilar plants

form an interesting arrangement when placed in the same coloured pots, even if the pots and the plants are different sizes.

Very large pots are now being produced in fibreglass, making them lightweight but strong. They come in amazingly convincing finishes including steel, lead, terracotta and stone and can incorporate hidden wheels and water reservoirs which work by capillary action.

For a dramatic effect, pots made of polyethylene in wonderful primary colours are available illuminated from within, creating a soft glow from an inbuilt light source. They are designed for inside or outside use and can look amazing – and not at all rustic!

Artwork and sculpture

Although the conservatory is not the right place for serious paintings or drawings – light levels will fade valuable pieces – it can be an opportunity to display sculptural pieces that have an organic quality. These don't need to be expensive – even simple collections of shells or fossils can look good. Museum postcards, inexpensively framed but with a horticultural theme, could form an interesting arrangement grouped on a shady wall, and they could all be replaced cheaply and easily if they become faded.

Museum shops can also be a good source of replica sculpture. These can look very convincing when displayed simply. Of course you may have some serious sculpture, which would work well in a conservatory, especially if sensitively lit. Beautiful things look best with plenty of space around them – resist the temptation to clutter up the place with too many little plants and allow the sculpture to be seen against the light from outside as well as inside.

The great strength of a conservatory is in being filled with light and beautiful views, so keep things simple. Don't fill it up with bits and pieces, be disciplined and remember William Morris's words: 'Have nothing in your houses that you do not know to be useful or believe to be beautiful'.

ABOVE A classic cast iron bench is perfectly placed below an antique urn in this period conservatory, lending it a romantic and nostalgic air.

RIGHT Groups of objects that are united by colour or shape and related to the garden, such as these sun hats and croquet mallets, make an attractive alternative to a sculpture or piece of art.

chapter six

conservatory gardening

Gardeners outdoors are facing increasingly unpredictable weather, and it can be hard to know which plants will do well in any given year. A conservatory is a controlled environment, so you can choose plants that you know will be well suited to the conditions and be much more confident of success. With an almost limitless range of plants available, you can also experiment with exotic species that you may not have come across before. This section provides an overview of what is possible and the best plants for different situations.

LEFT With the right ventilation and thermal controls, conservatories provide the perfect conditions for growing a huge range of plants, creating a calm oasis of green away from the rest of the house.

choosing plants

Conservatories are multi-functional rooms often used for informal living as well as for cultivating plants. This dual-usage can lead to problems, however, since many plants will not tolerate the warm, dry conditions most of us prefer. Choosing a few plants is a good start, and will enable you to gauge how to moderate the conditions so they are suitable for plants and humans.

ABOVE Two standard *Ficus benjamina* specimens are beautifully in proportion to the space in this dining room.

You need to decide from the start whether the conservatory is intended primarily as a place for growing wonderful plants, or as a comfortable living space. If the plants are the priority, you can regulate the temperature and humidity to suit the species you wish to grow, but most people prefer to limit the choice of plants to those that can tolerate the warm, dry air that feels best in a living room.

Even surprisingly large plants can survive in relatively small pots as long as they are regularly watered and fertilized, but may quickly become huge and top heavy given all the warmth and light. It is important, therefore, that you find out how big a plant may grow and how much care it will require before giving it a home.

Aspect and orientation

The direction the conservatory faces will be the major factor when deciding what species will be happiest growing there. Tender exotics will usually thrive in sunny spaces, while leafy plants, grown for their interesting or textural foliage, will generally prefer a more shady one. Some plants will be happy to be put out on terraces or decks in the summer and brought in when temperatures drop (though they do need to be acclimatized gradually to these changes), while others require year-round protection from the elements or do not tolerate being moved.

Planning and research

Plants can be bought from any number of sources, from supermarkets and garden centres to websites and specialist growers. The latter will be able to advise on the suitability, the problems and the best care, and a reputable nursery will often help if things go wrong. You can check the plants' individual needs in reference books and on the internet, or ask the nursery or specialist grower for detailed information.

It is sensible to choose plants that do not shed their leaves or are not horribly poisonous in a living environment, which rules out a surprising number of common plants. Plants that need to be kept in very humid conditions are also unsuitable in living room conditions, as are those that produce excess pollen, which can both make you sneeze and stain clothing. Some pollen is also poisonous. It can be useful to visit botanic gardens with specialist glasshouses for different species to see the sort of conditions certain plant groups prefer and to get an idea of what size they can eventually grow to given ideal conditions.

A general rule is that most plants prefer to be watered moderately and regularly, with time to dry out before the next watering, and be given filtered light and good air movement. More demanding plants, however, may require rainwater or filtered water, and some, including most edible species, require a lot of watering. If you know you will not be able to satisfy these needs then it may be an idea to opt for drought-tolerant plants, such as cacti, succulents and pelargoniums. Other types may be very fast growers that need to be cut back or repotted often, or require a lot of training, so you should bear this in mind too when choosing.

This chapter takes a closer look at a selection of plants suitable for different effects, from large plants and scented varieties to smaller types, fruit and vegetables. None of these are too demanding if you follow their care instructions and choose wisely.

TOP RIGHT If you use tap water, it is important to bring the container indoors to allow it to come up to room temperature before using it. Be aware that some plants will not tolerate tap water, however.

RIGHT A combination of different sized plants often works well. Here, smaller ones are raised up on delicate plant stands or grouped with vases, while large ones are in pots on the floor.

big leafy plants

Striking, architectural plants such as palms, bay trees, olive trees and members of the citrus family can add drama to a conservatory. Many grow quite big, so it is important to gauge how much space you have available, the type of pot you are going to use, and consider placing the pots on little wheels to help move them occasionally when cleaning the floor.

Palms are a traditional conservatory plant, redolent of romantic trysts in the Victorian era, and are reliable, forgiving and look good all year round. Suitable varieties are the Kentia palm, *Howea forsteriana*, or a pygmy date palm, *Phoenix roebelenii*. Find a specialist nursery, which will have a range of less well-known palms, and will advise you on the conditions they need, as well as (importantly) their ultimate height.

Ficus benjamina is a popular indoor tree, valued for its shiny green leaves and elegant weeping habit. In the right conditions it can grow to a great height, so be warned. Slightly prone to dropping its leaves if moved or shocked in some way – by a sudden change in temperature or by being waterlogged for instance – it is nevertheless well worth growing. Other members of the *Ficus* (fig) genus make good conservatory plants too, the easiest being *Ficus elastica*, the tough rubber plant that can withstand a lot of neglect.

Another impressive and suitably leafy plant to create a jungle feel in the conservatory is the elephant's ear or taro plant, *Alocasia macrorrhiza*. Its huge, glossy, shield-shaped leaves have a lovely texture and will transform your dining or living room into something more exotic, and may be all you need to convey the green message.

LEFT *Ficus binnendijkii* 'Alii' is a handsome small evergreen tree for a conservatory, but dislikes sudden change and may drop its leaves.

OPPOSITE Much loved by the Victorians, this Kentia palm looks perfectly placed by the fine cast iron spiral staircase in a period conservatory.

ABOVE A single *Schefflera* or umbrella tree can be all you need to create a jungle effect in a conservatory.

BELOW The muted greeny-grey hue of the olive tree is often chosen as the colour of conservatory paintwork.

Schefflera, the umbrella tree, is a popular indoor plant that can reach 2.4m/8ft tall given ideal growing conditions. Its large, glossy, compound leaves resemble an umbrella, as the name suggests, and make an instant bold statement.

The Japanese cycad or sago palm (*Cycas revoluta*) has a rugged trunk, topped with whorled feathery leaves, thus – like other cycads – looking very like a palm. It is, however, actually related to conifer and ginkgo trees – cone-bearing plants that trace their origins back to the ancient flora of the early Mesozoic era. Often called 'living fossils', cycads have changed very little in the last 200 million years. Given their durability, they should be infallible!

Elegant, fragrant members of the citrus family of fruit trees, such as oranges, lemons and grapefruit, look equally good in traditional or cutting-edge surroundings and have the added advantage of bearing edible fruit, although they need rather more attention and care than the previous suggestions. The combination of a pleasing compact form, scented flowers, shiny evergreen leaves and fruit makes for the ideal conservatory plant and they are well worth perservering with. Keep a close eye on them because they often suffer from scale insects, which can be hard to spot, being the same colour as the trunk of the tree they are attached to. The plants hate temperature change and will drop their leaves if this happens too suddenly; they are also easily killed by overwatering. Plenty of light, good ventilation and controlled watering and feeding keeps them happy.

Originating from the Mediterranean areas, olive trees (*Olea europaea*) have a graceful billowing habit and soft green-grey colour, and can make a delightful and trouble-free standard tree. The small, pale leaves cope well with drought conditions, are usually pest-free, and look wonderful in traditional or contemporary interiors. It is also a good tree to put out on to sheltered terraces during the warmer months, when fruit may form, although this may not be edible. In northern Europe the fruit does not usually ripen properly, but with climate change, who knows?

A small to medium-height, broadly conical evergreen tree, the bay (*Laurus nobilis*) is often clipped into a standard or 'lollipop' shape. It does well in pots, and is best taken outside when the danger of frosts is past. The leaves can be used in cooking, and it bears small, white, rather insignificant flowers. Although much loved by scale insects it is generally trouble free and is happy to be clipped back and kept in shape.

Sparrmannia africana, commonly known as African hemp, is a wonderful plant for a conservatory. Large, velvety, heart-shaped leaves held on delicate branches that allow the light to stream through them have, on close examination, tiny hairs that give an out-of-focus look to this sculptural variety. The small white flowers are charming, with long, yellow and red stamens. It requires indirect light and regular watering.

BELOW The large, soft, velvety leaves and attractive hairy stems of *Sparrmannia africana* provide an ethereal presence in filtered light all the year round, and make this a beautiful addition to a conservatory or garden room.

smaller plants

From hardy succulents and spring bulbs to the showy blooms of the tropical hibiscus, there is a huge range of smaller plants that are perfectly suited to conservatory conditions and that require very little care other than watering and the occasional feed.

RIGHT The pretty, scented white flowers and glossy leaves of *Coffea arabica* make this an interesting plant for the warm conservatory.

BELOW There are many different types of pelargonium to choose from, ranging from single-tone bright colours to white, pale pink and lovely duo-tone varieties. They make perfect conservatory plants since they have a long flowering period and require only minimal care.

Clivia miniata is named after the Duchess of Northumberland, Lady Charlotte Clive, who first cultivated the species in England in the mid-19th century. Usually producing stunning orange flowers in early spring, although there are white versions, this will grow well in warm shade. Strap-shaped leaves look good for the rest of the year. It likes moist, humus-rich soil – its natural habitat is on the forest floor – and a potash feed will encourage flowering.

Hibiscus rosa-sinensis is a tropical evergreen with large open flowers that is native to east Asia. Despite having very little scent, these amazing exotic blooms are often seen at shrines in India. They need plenty of warmth (not below 15°C/59°F) and sun (at least a few hours every day), meaning that the conservatory is the perfect location for them. Water using tepid rainwater and allow the soil to dry out between waterings. Although easy to grow, it can be prone to spider mites, so inspect the plant regularly.

An evergreen shrub or bush, *Coffea arabica* (coffee) has lovely glossy leaves and white, scented star-shaped flowers. The fruit contains two 'beans' but may take several years to ripen. It prefers filtered light and plenty of warmth, so plant in a shady corner of the conservatory. It requires regular watering, and feeding during the growing season. It may not provide you with plentiful coffee beans, but it is nevertheless a beautiful and unusual plant.

Grown for their colourful flowers or scented leaves, there are over 200 species of pelargonium to choose from and with colours ranging from dark inky claret to purest white, they will continue flowering for months. *Pelargonium crispum* has lemon-scented leaves, *P. tomentosum* has peppermint-scented leaves and both

make delightful conservatory plants, releasing their scent as one brushes past. They will grow in cool conservatories, but will not withstand frost. They prefer warmth, moderate watering and the occasional liquid fertilizer when in flower. They respond well to dead-heading to produce more flowers and are pretty undemanding, although they hate draughts. They can be put outside during the summer months.

Sometimes known as a Cape primrose, there are many varieties and colours of *Streptocarpus*. Pleasing crinkly leaves and an amazing facility to flower throughout the year makes this an essential house or conservatory plant, and those with white flowers are particularly beautiful. They seem quite happy in cool conservatories but prefer warm, light-filled areas. Feed with a high phosphate feed during their most active period and water moderately. In hot, dry atmospheres stand the pot on a tray of moist pebbles to raise humidity levels.

A vast genus of over 1,000 species, begonias are some of the most reliable plants, some grown for their extraordinary leaf markings, others for their flowers. Although sometimes overused in municipal planting schemes as summer bedding, begonias are one of the most trouble-free conservatory plants, and other than placing them out of full sun and watering occasionally, they require very little care. There are varieties for all tastes, ranging from trailing and tall cane varieties to camellia-shaped flowers in bright colours or pure white, as well as those with complicated crinkled and hairy foliage that looks good throughout the year.

Myrtus communis (myrtle) is a delightful small evergreen tree with white star-like flowers, a profusion of stamens and glossy aromatic leaves. The plant comes from the Mediterranean region, and is particularly associated with Aphrodite in Greek mythology. Sprigs of myrtle were traditionally woven into crowns for young women, and carried in wedding garlands, and it would make a pretty addition to a summer wedding design. The leaves and berries also have culinary and medicinal uses. Drought tolerant, this can be put outside during the summer, but must never be exposed to frost. It responds well to being clipped into shape and is often sold as a small mophead tree.

ABOVE Many garden plants can be grown in conservatories, and there is a huge range of shapes, colours and foliage to choose from. They look good on their own, or grouped with other plants, as demonstrated by this tasteful collection.

ABOVE The beautiful
Gladiolus X *colvillei* 'Albus' has
a neat habit, making it especially
suited to being planted in a pot
indoors, where it will produce a
wealth of stunning flowers.

RIGHT The intricate pineapple
lily, *Eucomis autumnalis* is a
welcome flower in late summer
and autumn, easy to grow with
fascinating stems and leaves
as a bonus.

Bulbs

Some of the most gratifying plants to grow in the conservatory, most bulbs require a period of cold, meaning that the main living area in a house is not necessarily suitable, but which the conservatory can provide. They require very little in the way of horticultural tending, and the sight of the first green tops appearing in spring is quite magical.

Especially good is the *Eucomis*, or pineapple lily. While not being difficult to grow in a sheltered garden, this relative of the hyacinth deserves observation at very close quarters, and does well in pots. A tuft of green bracts at the top of the inflorescences gives the plant the appearance of a pineapple and the tiny, quite odd flowers of a greeny purple/white are quite beautiful when seen close to. Lovely strappy leaves and speckled stems complete the interesting form of this plant. *E. autumnalis* and *E. pole-evansii* are the most interesting and somewhat scarce forms, which usually do well in a cool conservatory and can be put outside during the summer months.

Other good bulbs include *Cyrtanthus elatus* (syn. *Vallota speciosa*), which is a very reliable houseplant with stunning, bright red trumpet-shaped flowers, and *Gladiolus* X *colvillei* 'Albus', which has a compact form and produces a profusion of beautiful creamy flowers, although there are many different types that are suitable.

Hippeastrum is a spectacular plant and is grown both for its shape and its flowers. Many of these have been specially prepared for Christmas flowering, but those not designed for forcing will flower in spring, so you can extend the flowering period by choosing species carefully. Some varieties, such as *H. papilio* and *H. chico,* are strikingly unusual and make a welcome change from the more common ones found in the supermarket. Plant the bulbs in gritty, free-draining compost (soil mix) and keep them warm, well fed and moist but never overwatered.

Succulents

For those people who think they are not 'good with plants', succulents provide a good way to start. Because they store water in their fleshy leaves and stems, they can survive a little neglect. They prefer high levels of light and warmth and only moderate watering when the compost is completely dry. They hate cold draughts. Many succulents produce little offsets around the base of the plant which can be eased away and potted up, or leaf cuttings taken and the cut part pushed gently into a moist compost.

One of the best-known succulents, *Aloe vera* has a strong spiky architectural shape, is easy to grow and has special medicinal properties. The fleshy leaves contain a gel which can be squeezed out and put on to minor burns and grazes.

Aeonium 'Zwartkop' is an unusual tree-shaped succulent with plump rosettes of nearly black foliage. Stylish and architectural, it should be grown in free-draining potting compost (soil mix) with plenty of grit or sharp sand to aid drainage. Never let the compost become waterlogged, and keep the plant in bright filtered light.

Crassula ovata, also known as the jade tree, is a tree-like plant with plump fleshy leaves and star-shaped white flowers in the autumn; this succulent seems to thrive on neglect, and will

reward anyone who takes a moderate amount of care and attention by growing into what looks like an attractive old and gnarled small tree.

Echeveria is characterized by fleshy rosette-shaped leaves in soft bluey-green colours and a delicate white bloom, although *E*. 'Perle von Nurnberg' has beautiful purple leaves with paler edges. Spikes of little tubular flowers appear in early spring, but the leaves are what makes this plant so useful. To avoid damaging the leaves, water from below using the capillary method by placing in a shallow bowl of water until the compost is moist. Never allow these plants to remain standing in water or they will rot.

ABOVE Aloes add a sculptural desert feel to a conservatory. This *Aloe speciosa* looks particularly striking with its stunning red candelabra-shaped spires massed with tubular blossoms.

LEFT Natives of Madeira, black-purple *Aeonium* 'Zwartkop' bear striking rosettes at the end of their branches and make interesting conservatory plants.

planting for colour

Colour can lift the spirits, especially during the winter when the view outside is grey and the days are short. Many of the plants with strong colour come from Mediterranean or tropical countries, and these will often do well under glass in cold climates. They usually like warmth and high levels of light, making them better suited to sunny conservatories.

LEFT Pale blue plumbago is easy and rewarding to grow providing you keep the secateurs handy – it's rampant!

BELOW The glorious hot-pink, petal-like bracts of bougainvillea make a striking contrast to the blue paintwork in this conservatory.

When choosing plants, try to find out what the conditions are like in their native habitat. Then you can decide if they are suitable for your conservatory, and give them the soil, temperature, light and humidity levels they prefer. Many colourful plants can be simply grown in pots, but some require support against walls or trellis using vine eyes and wires, and will drop dead leaves and flowers, creating a little extra work. They will reward you, however, by creating an exotic ambience, sometimes with a glorious fragrance as well.

Colourful climbers

Bougainvillea, discovered by an admiral of the same name in Brazil, has spectacular papery coloured bracts (the real flower being a rather insignificant small white affair) and is a vigorous climber. In order to keep it flowering it is best kept quite dry and a little pot bound, but fed regularly with fertilizer. The leaves can drop if light levels are not high enough, and it is best suited to a conservatory or garden room where plants and their needs are the priority, rather than a general living space.

Mandevilla X *amoena* 'Alice du Pont' is a woody, twining evergreen vine with abundant, fragrant funnel-shaped pink flowers and rather sparse but glossy oval leaves. It prefers a well-draining, slightly sandy soil and filtered bright light and flowers prolifically during the summer, and to a lesser extent during the colder months. It is a vigorous climber that can grow to 6m/20ft and responds well to heavy pruning, and can be troubled by spider mites and white fly, so needs careful and regular inspection.

A glorious blue climber, native to South Africa, *Plumbago auriculata* does best in light, sandy soils with good drainage and bright light. Plumbago likes a slightly acidic pH. The foliage may turn yellow due to manganese deficiency in normal potting compost (soil mix), but applying some manganese sulphate will soon cure that. Water sparingly and allow to dry out between waterings.

Clerodendrum myricoides 'Ugandense', also known as the blue glory bower, is a really lovely evergreen climber from West Africa with blue to purple flowers and dark green, heart-shaped leaves. It prefers bright filtered light and plenty of warmth. It is best to let the soil dry between waterings. Deadheading frequently encourages new flowers to form.

Orchids

One of the largest and most diverse families of plants, orchids have beautiful and elegant flower forms. Once the preserve of the specialist collector, mass-produced new hybrids are now available from supermarkets. Despite their exotic looks, these improved varieties are not as delicate and temperature-sensitive as most people think.

Epiphytic, or 'air rooted', orchids can be found in the wild growing in the debris that collects in the forked branches of trees. In order to mimic these conditions in the conservatory, they need to be planted in a loose bark compost or osmunda fibre mixed with vermiculite, and like to be warm and a little humid. Misting with tepid rainwater in a small hand-held spray works well, or the pots can be positioned on moist pebbles or expanded clay granules to achieve a similar effect. Specialist orchid feed is available in concentrated liquid form, and can be used about once a month.

From the many types on offer, *Phalaenopsis*, or moth orchids, are especially beautiful. Other larger forms that do well are dendrobium hybrids, with their much larger flower heads, and cymbidiums, which are multi-stemmed. Both are suitable for the average conservatory and will flower for many weeks. Cymbidium orchids are also more robust than *Phalaenopsis*. They benefit from being put outside during the summer months to encourage flowering.

TOP *Phalaenopsis equestris*, with its lovely colouring of pale pink and magenta, makes a strong statement here.

ABOVE Morning glory thrives in warm conditions, the intense blue flowers lasting for just one morning, fading in the afternoon. New flowers appear each day.

planting for scent

Sometimes subtle, often pervasive, the scent of plants and flowers is a welcome addition to any conservatory. There are many varieties on offer, some of which are very beautiful to look at.

Several species of scented plant are perfect for growing in a pot in a conservatory, but many are climbers and require supports in the form of stakes, trellis or wires suspended from the wall or ceiling.

Among those that can simply be planted in a pot are *Michelia figo*, a medium-sized bush or small tree that bears magnolia-like cream or purple flowers with a wonderful scent, which thrives when given rainwater and regular feeding, and *Aloysia triphylla* or lemon verbena, which produces the most delectable lemony smell. The leaves can be made into a tisane or dried for pot pourri, and can also flavour jellies and desserts. It requires regular watering, and trimming when it becomes straggly.

Stephanotis floribunda, also known as Madagascar jasmine on account of its similarity in appearance to jasmine, is often sold as a house plant trained around a circle of wire, but it would be much happier climbing up a wall supported on wires. Planted in indirect sun, it produces elegant white waxy flowers with a wonderful scent, and glossy evergreen leaves, making it well worth growing. Water only when the soil is dry, and ensure it is free-draining. It also benefits from occasional misting and should be fed only during its growing season, not when it is flowering.

Hoya carnosa is a vigorous succulent climber with a beautiful scent and unusual waxy, star-shaped flowers of the palest pink. There are several different varieties and colours available, and they are easy to grow and propagate from stem. Flowers appear on plants after four years, but the end result is well worth the wait.

One of the most famous scented plants, jasmine is an evergreen climber with pretty white flowers that appear during late winter and early spring. It can become rampant, but responds well to hard pruning.

In addition to the beautiful common form of passion flower, *Passiflora caerulea*, you can choose one of the more exotic and colourful species, which are better suited to a conservatory. *P. quadrangularis* is a good choice, with large leaves, a delicious scent and stunning dark red flowers with purple corona filaments. A vigorous climber, it should be fed sparingly so it produces flowers rather than foliage.

ABOVE Pure white jasmine flowers give a heady scent which, combined with colourful plant leaves, makes it a good choice of climber.

RIGHT *Aloysia tryphylla* or lemon verbena releases a wonderful lemony smell when crushed, and can be used to make a tisane.

OPPOSITE *Passiflora caerulea* is the most common type of passion flower and it grows very well in conservatory conditions. It has a delicious scent and a wonderfully dramatic colour, making it a good choice of scented plant.

planting fruit and vegetables

The original purpose of conservatories was as a place for growing rare and tender fruit in cold climates, and the glass structures remain the ideal place to try your hand at growing a few types of fruit and vegetables, from lemons and limes to tomatoes, peppers, chillies and a range of delicious cut-and-come-again salad leaves.

BELOW A fruit-laden grape vine flourishes in this garden room. Good ventilation is needed to prevent Botrytis. Many vines are actually rooted outside the conservatory, the shoots trained to come in.

Although many varieties of fruit and vegetables will require rather more maintenance and specialist knowledge than other plants, that is all part of the challenge – and the pleasure. Many types have the advantage of being good-looking plants in their own right, with attractive flowers, so any edible offerings are an added bonus. Some growers offer collections of the small soft fruit trees described here, which can be moved out of the conservatory to make good additions to the terrace during warm weather.

OPPOSITE TOP Kumquats (*Fortunella japonica*) are attractive conservatory plants that are easy to look after. The fruits are normally eaten whole as the sweetness is in the skin.

OPPOSITE BOTTOM LEFT *Citrus sinensis limon*, with glossy evergreen leaves, scented flowers and wonderful lemons, makes the perfect conservatory plant.

OPPOSITE BOTTOM RIGHT Nothing smells or tastes better than tomatoes ripened on the vine, and conservatories provide ideal conditions. Plum tomatoes are sweet and very popular.

Fruit

Many types of citrus fruits grow especially well in conservatories, including oranges (*Citrus sinensis*), lemons (*C. limon*), grapefruit (*C.* × *paradisi*) and kumquats (*Fortunella japonica*). Plant in pots in a half and half mixture of loam and leaf compost and position in a sunny spot. Be aware that they require careful watering, as they hate either too much or too little water.

Grapes (*Vitis vinifera*) also do well when grown in conservatories. They do, however, require a good depth of soil, so you will need a large pot.

Most types of *Prunus persica* can be grown in conservatories, but the dwarf forms are especially suitable. *P. persica* 'Bonanza' is a dwarf peach with beautiful flowers and compact form. It can be grown indoors in a container and put outside on a terrace during warm summers. It will need a humus-rich, well-drained compost and plenty of sun, making it perfect for a sunny conservatory. Water when the compost has dried out and fertilize regularly.

The dwarf nectarine *P. persica* 'Nectarella' will reach a maximum height of 1.2–1.75m/4–5ft and will produce abundant fruit. It requires the same conditions as 'Bonanza'.

Prunus armeniaca 'Aprigold' is a small apricot tree that needs good strong light and warmth, and which can be taken out on to a terrace or sheltered part of the garden in summer.

Vegetables

Technically a fruit, tomatoes (*Lycopersicon esculentum*) are used as a vegetable. This aromatic plant is the perfect plant to grow in a warm conservatory, and the delectable fruits make a colourful addition to both the conservatory and the dinner table. There are many different varieties to choose from, with different flavours, colours and sizes, and all are packed with lycopene, a powerful antioxidant, as well as vitamin C. All types need warmth, plenty of

moisture and tomato feed, and most need careful training. There are some good dwarf varieties for smaller spaces, particularly 'Minibel' and 'Tumbler', and these look especially attractive when grown in a pot with some pungent basil.

From the same family as the tomato, *Solanum melongena* (aubergine/eggplant) does well in warm sunny situations and has the same requirements as tomatoes. Although it is not the most striking of plants, the fruit is so beautiful with its shiny skin and lovely shape that it is well worth growing. Take care when handling, however, as there are sharp prickles on the backs of the leaves. Calliope F1 hybrid is a good compact plant, without the spines, and has an interesting streaky colour.

There are many different types of the *Capsicum annuum* (pepper) and *Capsicum frutescens* (chilli pepper) to choose from, ranging from the various colours and sizes of bell pepper to the hot jalapeño pepper, and some varieties that are more ornamental than edible. Generally requiring well-drained soil and plenty of organic matter, they are from the same family as the tomato and aubergine (eggplant) and have very similar requirements.

Salad leaves

Seed producers sell cut-and-come-again salad mixtures for growing in a sunny kitchen conservatory. A wide variety of different leaf mixes are available, from pretty curly lettuce leaves in different colours, to spicy mesclun mixes with radicchio, rocket (arugula), endive, orach, mizuna, kale, mustard, and corn salad. These can be harvested after three or four weeks, and can be sown continuously in trays or containers throughout the year for a healthy salad.

Pick the young leaves in the morning, before the heat of the day sets in, and store in the refrigerator until mealtimes. Children in particular will enjoy growing these, and it is a good way to encourage them to try different types of leaves.

warm planting

For those living in northern Europe, the thought of being able to recreate the colour and scent of the warmer climes is irresistible and the conservatory provides ideal conditions for growing many plants that they would otherwise have difficulties with.

In temperate climates, plants that cannot tolerate frost, or the combination of winter wet and cold, can only be grown outdoors during the summer. A conservatory, especially a sunny one, enables you to keep many of these tender plants from year to year, either by growing them under cover all year round, or moving them inside for the winter.

Citrus fruits, olives and oleander are all popular Mediterranean plants, and in their native habitat are very tough and resilient. While they can be very successful in a conservatory, they often have problems if the conditions are not exactly right, and even in the best situations may suffer from insect pests. Perhaps the key to successfully growing all three is that they prefer very free-draining soil, need to dry out completely before being watered again, and relish long hours of sunlight and extended periods of warmth. Bougainvillea, seen everywhere in the Mediterranean, is a must, and provides long-lasting colour. It likes a sunny spot in the conservatory and regular feeding during the growing season.

Cacti and succulents also appreciate a warm conservatory, and the prickly pear, *Opuntia ficus-indica*, is a good sculptural addition, although care needs to be taken with the sharp spines and hairs, which can get under the skin and cause quite a lot of discomfort. Given the right conditions these produce a spectacular yellow/orange flower and even edible fruit; probably the best choice for anyone who tends to neglect to feed or water plants – these just thrive on it, and are easy to propagate.

ABOVE Sculptural cacti and succulents enjoy hot, dry conditions and require very little watering. They are ideal if you do not have much time to devote to your plants.

LEFT Pungent, pretty lemons will fill a warm, sunny conservatory with a lovely scent and provide a quintessentially Mediterranean atmosphere.

OPPOSITE Soft colours combine here to create a harmonious corner of a garden room. The blue-grey paintwork forms a good backdrop for the terracotta planter and the standard olive tree.

chapter seven

gardening techniques

Seeing your plants healthy and flourishing can be wonderfully rewarding, but it does require a little knowledge about how to look after them, and their varying requirements. Growing plants in a conservatory eliminates some of the common problems experienced outdoors – strong wind and rain, wildlife and birds – but they do still require some attention. This chapter covers the basic techniques required to maintain healthy plants as well as advice on propagation, pruning, and dealing with pests, diseases and other common problems.

LEFT The therapeutic value of growing and tending plants can be addictive, and with just a little know-how and a few basic pieces of equipment your garden room will soon be in full bloom.

back to basics

Having created an elegant, pristine and carefully considered conservatory, with good ventilation and heating, the plants that you have chosen need to be properly cared for in order to create a true indoor/outdoor oasis.

BELOW Examine plants carefully when buying. Choose ones with a healthy sheen to their leaves, plenty of new shoots and flower buds, and firm roots. Check stems for any sign of decay or infection, and water the plants well before repotting. These busy Lizzies are perfect specimens.

Whether you are using them as an architectural statement or to create a tropical jungle of climbers, conservatory plants will be dependent on you for all their needs. They tend to have fewer problems than other indoor plants, since they are likely to have all the light they need, but it can be difficult to keep them well watered – they can dry out very fast in the warm, sunny conditions. However, they will reward all your efforts, adding an extra dimension to the conservatory or sunroom.

Healthy plants

In an enclosed space with warmth and some humidity, it is inevitable that pests and diseases will thrive, so constant vigilance will be needed to nip them in the bud. In the natural environment there are plenty of creatures that live off insect pests, such as birds, frogs and other animals, but these are sadly not an option indoors. Choosing healthy plants in the first place is essential, and specialist nurseries can be a good place to source these, as knowledgeable staff are often happy to discuss the merits and pitfalls of each species and explain its needs.

When you buy plants, you should look for firm leaves without brown edges or spots and strong shoots and buds. Roots protruding from the base of the pot show the plant is ready to be potted on already and may have been under stress and starved of nutrition. Plants should not look leggy or sparse, and ideally will have a pleasing and balanced shape. Avoid any pot plants with leaves that look as though they have been nibbled – irregular shaped notches in the margins could be a sign of vine weevil, which will cause the plant to suddenly wilt and die without warning. The compost (soil mix) should be firm and the root system well established in the pot.

A great many tender tropical plants dislike change; a draught and a drop in temperature or light levels will cause leaf drop and wilt, with yellowing leaves or buds dropping off. This is usually temporary as long as they are quickly restored to the right conditions, but do try to establish them in the conservatory as soon as possible and allow them to acclimatize.

Cleaning

Keeping the conservatory clean is really important, not just for aesthetic reasons, but because fallen leaves can harbour insects and mould without one noticing. It may be a good idea to have large pots or planters on wheeled bases so that they can be gently and easily moved for sweeping up dead leaves lurking behind and in corners.

Temperature and ventilation

Many houseplants prefer a daytime temperature of 18–21°C (64–70°F), although some plants require a cooler temperature during their dormant phase in late autumn and winter. Good ventilation will prevent a build-up of heat and humidity, which can enable pests and diseases to thrive and have an adverse effect on some species. Opening windows improves air circulation but this can also let in cold draughts, which some plants don't like. Finding the right balance is difficult, so invest in a device with a digital readout, showing inside and outside temperatures as well as relative humidity.

OPPOSITE TOP This grasshopper is not a pest and is welcome in the conservatory, but look out for less friendly passengers when buying plants.

ABOVE Keeping the conservatory clean and tidy will minimize organic matter that provides hiding places for insects and moulds.

watering and feeding

It is very important that plants are given the right amount of water and food, and that the humidity levels around them are correct. Species have different needs, so it is worth taking the time to do a little research to ensure they remain healthy.

TOP Water is best poured over the soil rather than the foliage.

ABOVE Some plants prefer to soak up water from below. This works with porous terracotta pots positioned in a saucer.

Many conservatory plants come from tropical countries, with high light levels, warmth and occasional downpours of rain. In between downpours, the soil dries out. In order to keep your tropical plants healthy, you should mimic these conditions by giving the plant a good drench and then allowing excess water to drain through and the soil to dry out before delivering more.

Rainwater, served at room temperature, is ideal for most plants, and it is a good idea to keep a watering can or bucket of rainwater on hand in the conservatory. Not only does this ensure the water is at the correct temperature, but it also makes the air a little humid, which is good for the plants. Try and avoid using freshly drawn tap water: it will probably be too cold, and contains chemicals which are harmful to many plants – though some are more tolerant than others. If you have to use tap water, let it sit and become tepid and allow the chlorine to evaporate before using.

There are various ways of providing plants with the water they need, and the method used depends on their position and what sort of container they are planted in. These include:

- **Top watering** Slowly pour water from a can on to the soil rather than over the leaves and flowers, allowing the water to penetrate the compost (soil mix). If you add the water too quickly it may simply run down the side between the dry compost and the pot. A small watering can with a long fine spout can be useful for this. Do not allow plants to sit in saucers of water; pour off any excess once the pot has drained through.
- **Bottom watering** Fill the saucer that the pot is positioned on with water. Empty the saucer when the surface of the compost is damp.
- **Sub-irrigation** Stand the pot in a sink or bowl with water halfway up the pot. Remove the pot when the moisture has 'wicked' upward through the compost and the surface looks moist.
- **Plunge watering** Submerge the pot (but not the whole plant!) into a bucket of water until the compost is moist but not waterlogged, then allow the surplus water to drain out over the bucket.
- **Capillary matting** Place pots of plants on a piece of capillary matting with a wick leading to a large trough of water. This will draw up moisture, keeping the mat and, in turn, the plant roots, moist. This simple system is extremely useful for supplying moisture to your plants when you are away from home.

Misting and humidity

Many tropical plants benefit from fine misting to aid humidity. Orchids in particular appreciate this. Using a small spray bottle, lightly spray the foliage in the evening, preferably with rainwater at room temperature. Tap water can leave white spots of calcium on the leaves in hard water areas.

A more effective way to achieve a constant high level of humidity is to place the pots on a tray of expanded clay granules or small pebbles on to which water has been poured. As the water evaporates, it will provide the necessary humidity. Grouping plants together can also raise humidity levels as they create their own microclimate too. However, if the air is too humid, mould will appear on leaves and drought-loving plants will show patches of rot. Destroy any affected areas because moulds are airborne and quickly spread. Tell-tale signs of inadequate humidity levels are buds falling off or not opening, leaves turning yellow and drooping or turning brown at the tips.

Feeding

Plants in pots can quickly exhaust the nutrients in their compost, especially in a warm, sunny conservatory where they may be growing rapidly, so they will need some fertilizer from time to time during their growing season.

- **Liquid feeds** Usually sold in concentrated form, these are possibly the best way to feed plants. They should be used according to directions on the manufacturers' label, and be added slowly on to the soil with water to allow it to be distributed evenly throughout the pot. The three main ingredients for most plant feeds are nitrogen, phosphorus and potassium, in varying ratios.
- **Slow-release granules** These are especially handy as they can be added to the compost when re-potting. They can be also sprinkled over the top of existing compost and watered in. Little sticks of solid slow-release fertilizer are also available and work best if directed towards the root ball, but they may concentrate the nutrients too much in one area.
- **Other feeds** Orchids and citrus plants have special requirements and their fertilizer is available from good nurseries and garden centres. If in doubt, check the feeding requirements in the directory, or look on the internet.

TOP Plants 'breathe' through their leaves, so keeping them clean and clear of dust or limescale spots not only makes them look better, but keeps them healthy and makes it easier to check for pests.

MIDDLE Plants may be grouped together to raise humidity levels, and as shown here, placed on damp expanded clay granules which increase humidity but don't allow the plants to become waterlogged.

RIGHT Essential nutrients in the potting compost will need to be replenished by applying liquid or solid plant food during the plant's growing period. Always follow the instructions on the packet.

composts and potting

Most plants bought at nurseries and garden centres come in small plastic pots with the roots already trying to escape through the bottom. At some stage after you buy them, they will need to be potted on into a larger pot with fresh potting compost.

ABOVE You will need to pot on plants when you first buy them and as they outgrow successive pots. This is a chance to check the roots for signs of rot or vine weevil, and to add some appropriate slow-release fertilizer to the potting compost.

RIGHT Different plants require different types of compost, so it is well worth checking this when you buy the plant. Cacti, succulents, orchids, and bromeliads in particular require specialist compost and the correct conditions to thrive.

The first thing you should do after bringing plants home is to carefully check them before bringing indoors and exposing them to the healthy plants in your conservatory. Gently ease the plant out of its pot or packaging and have a look to see whether there are signs of vine weevil among the roots, a pest that has become rampant in recent years. The plant may show no sign of disease until it suddenly flops in the pot and a colony of white grubs with brown heads are found to have attacked the roots or bored into bulbs and rhizomes.

Potting composts

Choosing the right potting compost (soil mix) is vital to plant health. Garden soil is unsuitable, containing weed seeds as well as pests and diseases that may not be evident to the naked eye. There are two main types of potting compost: loam-based and soil-less. Sand or grit can be added to both these mixes to improve drainage.

Loam-based potting composts are more like garden soil, but are broken down into a fine mixture and sterilized. They usually contain added fertilizers and hold moisture well. Their weight will also help to hold the plant firmly in place and stabilize the pot. Soil-less potting composts are traditionally based on peat, but this is environmentally unfriendly, so choose peat-substitute potting composts. However, peat-based and peat-substitute potting composts tend to dry out more easily. Once they have dried out, they are harder to rehydrate than loam-based mixes.

Certain plants need specialist growing mediums, usually available from specialist nurseries and good garden centres. Some orchids and bromeliads, for example, are epiphytic, which means they grow on tree branches, where there is very little that resembles soil. They need a special, low-nutrient compost, and a transparent pot, since the roots need light for photosynthesis. Cacti and succulents also do better in a special cactus potting compost.

potting up

1 Fill the bottom of a clean, scrubbed pot with drainage material, such as broken pieces of old terracotta pot or small stones, covering the drainage holes.

2 Cover with a good layer of fresh potting compost (soil mix) and tap this down to remove any air pockets. Position the plant about 2cm/¾in below the rim of the pot to allow space for watering.

3 Add potting compost around the sides of the rootball and tap down again.

4 Continue this process until the potting compost is packed firmly around the rootball, pushing down with your thumbs to leave a firm surface for watering. Water in well. A fertilizer stick can be inserted into the potting compost.

Potting up, potting on and repotting

There are several different types of potting: potting up, which is what happens the first time a seedling or cutting is given its own pot; potting on, which is the action of replanting the rootball in a larger pot; and repotting, which means replacing the plant in a pot of the same size, but with most of the potting compost replaced. All use the same technique, shown above, although there are other methods.

Never be in a hurry to pot on plants into a larger container: root disturbance will result in some check to growth. However, you shouldn't pot on into a much larger pot in order to reduce the frequency of potting on. Roots always go straight to the bottom before moving sideways, so a plant will produce a greater quantity of useful roots in its limited space if the pot size is increased gradually. Young plants require potting on much more frequently than older ones as they grow more rapidly.

Top dressing

Mature plants may not need potting on, but may have exhausted their potting compost. Scrape off the top layer of old compost, as much as you can without disturbing the roots. Replace with fresh potting compost. Water in well with a liquid fertilizer or add slow-release fertilizer.

BELOW Adding a top dressing of fresh compost and some slow-release fertizer granules will provide extra nourishment to the plant in the short term before finally having to repot.

propagation

Plants are programmed to propagate themselves. As well as producing seeds, many have evolved so that a leaf or piece of stem that is accidentally broken off will root and form a new plant if it lands in a favourable spot. Gardeners take advantage of this phenomenon by taking cuttings, using a variety of techniques to give the plants ideal conditions for taking root.

BELOW You should always use the tip of a plant for soft cuttings if possible. Check that the parent plant is absolutely healthy and well-watered to give the shoot the best chance.

You can take cuttings at almost any time of the year, using different techniques. Take soft cuttings in the late winter and spring; semi-ripe cuttings in the summer; and woody cuttings in the autumn. It is also possible to take soft cuttings in the autumn by cutting back plants in the late summer and allowing them to shoot again. Ensure all cutting material used is short-jointed and free from any disease or infestation, and choose only material from strong and healthy growing plants.

Soft cuttings

Depending on your location, climate and conservatory conditions, take soft cuttings in the late winter or spring when plants are growing strongly. Different parts of the shoot can be used as cuttings, but it's always best to use a tip cutting, if you have enough material. The tip contains the highest concentration of natural growth hormones and it will root more quickly. It also gives a more symmetrical cutting, with the flexibility to be trained and grown on in different ways.

Before you start, ensure the parent plant is well watered. Cut just below a node with a razor-sharp knife to give a cutting with two sets of leaves and a growing tip. Handle it by the leaves if possible, to avoid bruising the stem. Cut off the bottom set of leaves, dip the end in rooting powder, if you like, and immediately place the cutting into a pot of moist, free-draining compost (soil mix). Add a label. If you have a propagator, you can put the cuttings inside, with a bottom temperature of 15–21°C/60–70°F. If not, you could enclose the pot in a plastic bag, held away from the plants with sticks, but many cuttings will do better uncovered, so try some with each method. Keep the cuttings in good light, but not in direct sunlight, until they root. When rooted the cuttings will start to make new tip growth. At this point, gradually increase the ventilation, if you have covered them, to acclimatize the cuttings to the drier outside air and harden them off.

Semi-ripe cuttings

In the summer, stems have started to ripen. Take a longer cutting with a 'heel' (a lump where you have torn a side shoot off the main stem), up to five pairs of leaves and the growing tip. Remove all flower buds, treat the bottom node and stem with fresh rooting powder or gel, and then treat as soft cuttings.

taking cuttings

1 Using a sharp knife, remove a suitable cutting from its parent plant.

2 Add some coarse grit or sand, and/or vermiculite or perlite, to the compost (soil mix) to improve drainage, if you like.

3 Fill small pots or cells with the mixture. Remove the lower leaves from the stem and insert into a prepared hole in the compost. Add a label to each pot or cell.

4 Water with a spray, or a watering can with a fine rose. Place in good light, in a propagator or plastic bag, if you like.

Hardwood cuttings

In the late summer and autumn, when the wood is ripe, it is possible to take hardwood cuttings with a heel. To do this, tear off a whole side shoot with a heel of bark from the parent stem. Remove any flowers or buds, and treat similarly to soft cuttings.

Offsets and plantlets

Plants such as cacti and succulents, as well as bromeliads, produce offsets or baby plants at the base. Once the offsets start to resemble the parent plant, remove them with a sharp knife and plant the offset into a very free-draining compost (soil mix). This should be kept moist in order to start them off. Cactus and succulent cuttings should be left to dry for day or so before planting.

A few houseplants, such as spider plants (*Chlorophytum comosum*), produce plantlets at the ends of trailing runners, while the pick-a-back plant (*Tolmeia*) has plantlets on its leaves. If the plantlets already have small roots, then they can be planted up in potting compost. If they don't have roots, then they can be held down on the potting compost with a bent hair-pin or paper clip until the roots have formed and are able to anchor the plant down.

OPPOSITE Soft cuttings should take root in 28 days and make new tip growth.

ABOVE RIGHT Bromeliads, like cacti and succulents, produce offsets.

RIGHT Spider plants produce plantlets that can be very easily propagated.

pruning

'Shaping' is probably a better word than 'pruning' when it comes to describing the needs of most plants that are grown in conservatories, although some vigorous plants do need cutting

TOP Remove spent flowers from plants. This not only improves their appearance but encourages more flowers.

ABOVE Pinching out the leading shoots of a plant will encourage bushy growth. It can be done with your fingers or using small scissors.

When growing plants in a conservatory you need to restrict their size to suit the space and the pot they are planted in. Straggly indoor shrubs, dead leaves littered on the floor and spilt potting compost (soil mix) not only look messy, but they can also harbour pests and diseases.

If your plants are growing lopsided, it is not always necessary to prune them back into shape. Simply turning the pots a quarter turn every week will encourage uniform growth, as well as exposing all sides of the plant to light, resulting in improved general health.

Whenever you prune, you need to ensure that the tools you use are sharp and clean so you get a good cut and don't risk spreading infection. Garden scissors or small secateurs (hand pruners) are ideal – use whatever is most comfortable for you. After use, always ensure you wipe the blades clean to prevent the spread of disease and to stop them going rusty. Store all tools somewhere safe, out of reach of children and animals.

There are several methods of pruning indoor plants, none of which require the more heavy-weight equipment used for pruning their tougher outdoor cousins:

• **Dead-heading** Remove any flowers that are past their best with your fingers or scissors – this will encourage the plant to produce more.

• **Pinching out** You can encourage some plants to bush out by pinching out the leading shoots, resulting in new growth lower down the stem. To do this, pinch or cut away the ends of stems that have several sets of leaves on them, just above the joint of the stem from which the shoot starts to grow (known as the node).

• **Cutting back** If a plant outgrows its space, cut it back using secateurs. This is best done in late winter or early spring, but with spring-flowering plants you can leave it until after they have flowered, otherwise you will lose that season's flowers. If climbing plants become straggly, cut back slightly after flowering and tie in wayward shoots. Bend them sideways and downwards to encourage bushiness and flowering lower down.

• **Root pruning** This is a more drastic form of pruning for larger plants that are outgrowing their pots. Remove the plant from its pot and trim off the root tips, making sure you leave at least two-thirds of the root system intact. Return the plant to its pot, packing in extra compost to take up the space left by the removed roots. Remove about two-thirds of the top growth at the same time.

common problems

Most problems associated with plants grown in conservatories and sunrooms are due to lighting levels, over- or underwatering, or incorrect temperatures. As a result plants may become stressed, making them more susceptible to pests and diseases.

Many plants succumb to stress at some point and, although they may look beyond redemption, most can be restored to full health reasonably easily. As with everything, however, prevention is always better than cure, so be vigilant and spot signs of distress early on so you can deal with them quickly.

- **Upper leaves turn yellow** Often the result of watering lime-hating plants with hard tapwater. Use cooled boiled or filtered water, or rainwater. Try using a proprietary feed formulated for acid-loving plants.
- **Flower buds dropping off or not opening** Could be caused by insufficient light and/or humidity, or lack of water.
- **Brown spots and patches on leaves** Could be caused by too much sunlight scorching the leaves, by drops of water on sensitive leaves, or insects. Move the plant out of strong sunlight and inspect the underside of the leaves. If insects are discovered, try brushing or rubbing them off, or use an insecticide if the infestation is severe.
- **Leaves curling at the edges and dropping off** Possibly caused by the plant being positioned in a cold draught, or by overwatering. Some insects can also have this effect.
- **Leaves with brown tips and/or edges** This is caused by a lack of humidity or by the plant being too hot. It can also be caused by tapwater, which contains chemicals, so try using rainwater, filtered water, or cooled boiled water. Remove the leaves because they will not recover.
- **Wilting leaves** A sign of either underwatering or overwatering. May also be caused by vine weevil, which feed on roots. If you find a bad infestation, throw away the whole plant immediately.
- **Sudden leaf fall** Single leaves fall off all the time, but if all the leaves fall off, then the plant has had a shock – extreme cold or heat, complete dehydration, or waterlogging. The weeping fig (*Ficus benjamina*) is prone to this.
- **Rotting leaves or stems** A sign of overwatering and poor drainage which encourages grey mould to grow. Remove affected parts, improve the air circulation around the plant and spray with carbendazim.
- **Yellow patches between veins of leaves** Can be caused by magnesium deficiency, which is easily treated by a dose of diluted Epsom salts (20g/¾oz per 1 litre/1¾ pints water) and with a foliar feed. Follow the manufacturer's instructions.

TOP Remove leaves with brown edges or tips or which have died altogether with secateurs (hand pruners) or small scissors.

ABOVE Most leaf wilt is due to inaccurate watering, so check the soil regularly to see if it is too dry or too wet.

pests and diseases

No matter how clean you keep your conservatory and how carefully you tend your plants, everyone at some point is likely to have to deal with pests and diseases, whether they fly in or are brought in with new plants, which is why it is important to keep a close eye on plants.

Healthy, well-nourished plants will be less likely to succumb to disease, but it is inevitable that the occasional damage from strong sunlight or physical damage will provide the perfect opportunity for fungal infection or insect damage to take hold. Dead leaves and flower heads are good hiding places too, and it is important that you keep the place clean and tidy. Old pots should be scrupulously cleaned and sterilized before re-use, as should any tools used on infected plants, to prevent the spread of infection.

A clean start

Start with the soil. Never be tempted to use garden soil; instead always use sterile potting compost (soil mix) from a reputable source. Garden earth teems with micro-organisms, some of them beneficial, many of them unwelcome in the conservatory. When buying potting compost, match the compost to the needs of the plant. A free-draining loam-based compost works for most plants, but a little homework is needed before planting more exotic specimens. Always buy the best compost, which may have a numbering system to denote suitability for different applications. Compost is also available which contains thiacloprid for vine weevil control.

Dealing with pests

There are many different types of pests that can afflict indoor plants, but here is a list of some of the most common, and advice on how to deal with them. Always read manufacturers' labels and follow the usage instructions carefully, and wherever possible, take plants outside to be treated.

- **Aphids** Tiny green or black sap-sucking insects that cluster round leaf stems and tips. They leave behind a sticky substance, sometimes known as honeydew, which can become infected with black sooty mould. A strong jet of water may remove enough to limit the damage, if done regularly. Otherwise, you can spray with an insecticidal soap, or a chemical control. Pirimicarb is an aphid-specific one. Aphids may spread viruses and weaken plants, but rarely kill them.
- **Whitefly** Clouds of very small white winged insects, these reproduce very quickly and are becoming resistant to insecticides. They love warm conservatories and greenhouses, so are something to watch out for. The adults and their whitish-green, scale-like nymphs feed on sap from the undersides of

the leaves, which weakens the plant, and the sticky honeydew they secrete encourages the growth of moulds. One quite effective way of trapping them is by positioning sticky yellow sheets around the affected plants. Small parasitic wasps, *Encarsia formosa*, are available by mail order, but these are not a suitable option where the conservatory is an integral part of the living space. You can spray with an insecticidal soap or a chemical insecticide.

- **Vine weevils** The adult is a brownish-grey beetle that bites semicircles into the edges of leaves. If you are not squeamish, pick them off and crush them. They are easier to spot in the evening as they tend to hide during the day. The unseen danger is the fat white grubs or larvae that are found at the bottom of the pot and which feed on the roots, causing sudden and catastrophic wilt and death. If this happens, dispose of the plant and surrounding soil immediately. One control of the larvae is available as microscopic pathogenic nematodes, *Steinernema kraussei* or *Heterorhabditis megidis*, which can be obtained from suppliers by post, and watered into the compost in late summer. The larvae are quite resistant to chemical controls.

- **Red spider mite** You will need a magnifying glass to see this mite and its white eggs on the underside of leaves, which may have a yellow mottling. There may also be a fine silky webbing. It causes the leaves to dry up and fall off until only shoot tips remain. Despite its name, the mite is yellowish-green, only becoming orange-red in autumn and winter. To treat, spray with insecticidal soap or a chemical control. Dispose of badly affected plants carefully. Spraying under leaves with water and keeping humidity high will discourage the pests.

Dealing with diseases

A disease is usually the symptoms caused by a small parasite that attacks a plant's cells. They are usually caused by fungi, bacteria or viruses, and by the time symptoms become obvious, they may have already caused substantial damage.

- **Grey mould** This greyish white fuzzy growth on leaves and stems is caused by the fungus *Botrytis cinerea* and is especially prevalent in very humid conditions. The airborne spores only usually infect healthy plants via cuts or tears. It thrives in dead matter and can remain dormant in plant tissue for months. Improve the circulation of air to the conservatory and remove badly affected plants immediately.

- **Anthracnose** Causing leaves to turn yellow then dark brown and eventually die, this disease is caused by the fungi *Colletrotrichum* and *Gloeosporium*, which enter the plant via wounds. Destroy any affected leaves and avoid misting the plant.

- **Powdery mildew** The formation of a white, powdery growth or dry, brown, papery leaf spots is caused by the fungus *Oidium* species. Improve air circulation and avoid overwatering, and remove any badly affected leaves.

TOP Vine weevil grubs feed on the roots of plants.

MIDDLE Red spider mite can be seen with a magnifying glass.

ABOVE Grey mould is common in conservatories.

late winter/early spring to-do list

In the garden, the unpredictable weather often causes problems at this time of the year – new growth, encouraged by warm temperatures, can be damaged by late frosts. The conservatory is a protection from these dangers, but you still need to be more aware of the changing weather.

TOP Clean, sparkling windows make all the difference in a conservatory, especially when the sun is low in the sky.

ABOVE Thorough cleaning of all pots, surfaces and tools prevents the risk of cross-contamination and looks better.

RIGHT Label seeds carefully when you sow them and tie in any unruly stems.

As the evenings start to grow lighter and temperatures rise slightly, it is time to take stock of the plants in your conservatory and think about the growing season to come. This simple checklist will ensure that you do all the little things that will ensure your plants remain happy and healthy throughout the year.

• With low sunlight, windows show every smear, so make sure they are sparkling.

• Check all plants closely for signs of disease or damage and cut out any diseased or dead leaves and stems.

• Pot on any plants which have outgrown their pots.

• Some plants can root from cuttings almost any time, but spring is by far the best for most indoor plants.

• Cuttings taken at the end of the previous year will now need to be put into larger pots. Always use scrupulously clean pots and fresh compost (soil mix), and then water in with tepid (preferably rain) water. Take off any dead flower heads and damaged leaves from mature plants and trim off any unruly shoots.

• Start gradually feeding and watering plants again, with the appropriate fertilizer, after their winter rest, and watch out for dry or compacted compost.

• Start sowing seeds for aubergines (eggplants), tomatoes and peppers. Herbs can also be sown from seed – lemon grass would be worth trying along with French tarragon and sweet basil, which both need shelter and warmth. Remember to label them carefully – seedlings look much the same when they first appear. Cut-and-come-again salad seeds can be planted – cut the baby leaves when they have reached about 10cm/3in high and they will shoot up again within a few weeks if kept well watered.

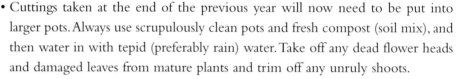

• Check for signs of aphids and whitefly.

• Order bulbs for autumn flowering – try to grow some of the more tender plants that would be difficult to grow outside, such as nerines and crinums.

• Watch weather reports for cold nights and frosts, which might affect tender plants on windowsills, as they will need moving away from the glass.

late spring/early summer to-do list

It may be tempting to simply sit back and enjoy the view in this glorious season, but this is the time when you need to feed and water your plants more and be very alert to pests,

Late spring and early summer tasks are all about watering, feeding and vigilance and it is also the ideal time to introduce new plants to your conservatory.

- Check that plants are getting enough air circulating around them by moving them a little apart, and ensure that they are shaded from scorching direct sun. Even on chilly days the sun can make the conservatory quite hot.
- Many plants can be safely put outside on a terrace when all danger of frost is past, although not those that need a constant temperature both day and night.
- Feeding with liquid fertilizer can generally be done every two weeks.
- Keep the tops of pots free from any fallen leaves or dead flowers as pests and moulds can take over and colonize. Remove dead flower heads to encourage more flowers. Producing seed uses a lot of the plant's energy, and once allowed to, they will reduce or stop flowering.
- Train new shoots of climbers over wires in the direction you want them to grow, and trim any that are getting out of hand or that spoil the shape. Do the training before the trimming in case shoots get damaged.
- Check large plants are not drying out – those with large expanses of leaves lose water through transpiration and can dry out very quickly on hot days. They may need water twice a day, or even more often.
- Check plants for pests and diseases. If your conservatory forms part of the living area, take plants outside if possible and spray a control. There are now biological controls for most pests and many that are simply watered on do the task very efficiently.
- If you plan to go away, group plants together – they benefit from the humidity – or in a shaded corner with filtered light, with the bigger sun-loving plants shading the more delicate ones. Stand smaller pots on capillary matting with one end in a tank of water. Large pots will not be able to draw up sufficient water by this method, so give them a soaking before you go, and try burying a capillary tape in the pots – or ask a neighbour to water them.

TOP Some plants benefit from being put outside when all danger of frosts is past.

ABOVE There is nothing to replace feeling the compost with your hands to ensure the plant is neither too wet nor too dry.

LEFT Group plants together in a shaded corner when you go away, and arrange some form of watering.

late summer/early autumn to-do list

This is the season in which the conservatory really comes into its own, and you can enjoy the fruits of your labour in a sweetly scented and beautiful room. Plan for next year and take cuttings from healthy plants, which can be nurtured indoors until the spring.

ABOVE Tomatoes require regular watering as the fruits ripen.

ABOVE RIGHT Spring bulbs should be bought at this time.

BELOW Seedlings prosper in the shelter of a conservatory.

Ventilation and temperature control are especially important during hot weather, and it is vital that you monitor both or your plants will suffer. Try to open windows and doors as much as possible, but keep an eye out for unwanted visitors who may view the room as a larder.

• Aubergines (eggplants), tomatoes and pepper plants will need regular feeding and watering, as will soft fruits such as peaches and apricots.

• Keep a careful eye out for pests such as spider mites, which love the dry conditions and the profusion of plant materials.

• Late summer is a good time to take pelargonium cuttings. Choose a healthy looking shoot and make a clean cut just below a leaf joint. Remove lower leaves and plant the cutting in a small pot of free-draining compost (soil mix). Several shoots can be put in the same pot. Water well and put in a cool place.

• Cuttings can be taken from other conservatory plants such as hibiscus and passion flowers in much the same way as described above, but the shoots may need to be dipped in a hormone powder to encourage rooting. Water well, then put the small pot and cutting into a plastic bag to create a mini greenhouse, keeping the cutting clear from the sides of the bag. Secure the bag around the pot with a rubber band. After a few weeks, remove the bag and check for signs of new growth.

• Spring bulbs often start to appear in garden centres and grower's catalogues in early autumn, so now is a good time to have a look at catalogues. Many bulbs are sold ready prepared for forcing into flower around Christmas and can be planted in bulb fibre in a decorative pot as a present. These will need to be kept in a cool dark place, not the conservatory, until the new shoots are about 3cm/2in high, then bring them into the light and water well. Hippeastrum, hyacinth and narcissus can all be grown in this way and will give pleasure during the short dark days of winter.

• Autumn is a good time to pot up a few herbs from the garden for use indoors. Dig up some stalks of mint with the roots attached and pot up – an easy way to prolong the season.

late autumn/early winter to-do list

Many plants are pretty much dormant during the coldest and darkest months of the year, and only need feeding and watering occasionally. Others can provide some colour and cheer, and it is worth considering these plants when planning your planting.

There are winter days when the sun shines and the weather is quite mild, only to be followed by freezing temperatures, dark skies and constant rain. Low light levels may affect some plants, but others such as cyclamen and orchids happily brighten dark days and provide colour.

• Water sparingly during this period and reduce liquid feeding to once a month if necessary.

• Aubergine (eggplant) seeds can be sown in late winter by first soaking the seeds for two days before sowing singly into small pots filled with seedling compost. Baby salad leaf seed collections can be planted at any time.

• Plant *Eucomis* (pineapple lily) bulbs for later summer/autumn flowering. *E. bicolor* or *E. autumnalis* are especially delightful, with greeny white flowers, good strappy leaves and a rather amusing pineapple of small green bracts on top.

• Buy seeds from specialist suppliers for bringing on before planting in the garden. Involve children in learning how to plant and care for plants.

• This is a good time to read about plants. Look critically at what you have grown in previous months and consider whether they look good together, or whether you have created a random mix of unrelated plants. For inspiration, visit some of the great conservatories and botanic institutes to see what species grow together in harmony, enjoying the same climate conditions.

ABOVE Phalaeonopsis or moth orchid will flower for months and look elegant and exotic.

BELOW Baby lettuce leaf collections can be cut a few weeks after sowing and provide a fresh and tangy salad, grown without chemicals.

RIGHT A small packet of seeds can provide dozens of seedlings. It is immensely satisfying to raise your own plants from seed, for gifts or just for your own pleasure. The conservatory provides the ideal conditions for raising tender seedlings, since it is warm and light and protected from the elements.

chapter eight

plant directory

Whether you enjoy propagating from seed or cuttings or simply love the colour and form that plants bring to the conservatory, there is a plant to suit every taste. Growing plants are so much better value than buying cut flowers, can provide some of the ingredients for a meal at little cost, and help purify the air. They teach children about the growth cycle, nature and nurture, and probably insect life too. A conservatory without a plant would seem a contradiction in terms. The list of suitable plants is endless, but here are a few that work well.

LEFT Hot colour for a hot fruit! These *Capsicum annuum* Longum Group, or chilli peppers as they are commonly known, grow happily in the conservatory and are evergreen.

Aeonium 'Zwartkop'

Agave americana

Allium schoenoprasum

Aloe ferox

Acacia dealbata
Mimosa

A fast-growing tree with fluffy yellow ball-shaped, scented flowers and feathery glaucous leaves. The branches will need pruning after the flowering period.
Light Full sun.
Temperature Cool to warm.
Watering and feeding Keep moist when in growth and reduce watering in winter. Apply a liquid fertilizer every fortnight during the summer.
Cultivation Requires free-draining neutral to acid soil.

Aeonium 'Zwartkop'

This tree-shaped succulent has rosettes of fleshy, nearly black foliage.
Light Bright/filtered.
Temperature Cool to warm.
Watering and feeding Keep moist when in growth and reduce watering in winter. Never

let the compost (soil mix) become waterlogged. Apply a liquid fertilizer occasionally when in full growth.
Cultivation Pot on in spring, using a free-draining potting compost containing grit or sharp sand.

Agave

Some species of this succulent can grow huge in the wild, but they will remain a manageable size in pots. Mature plants may produce flower spikes indoors, but they are generally regarded as foliage plants. *A. americana* has large, blue-grey, lance-shaped leaves, with sharp spines. As a pot plant, it is usually grown in one of its variegated forms, such as 'Marginata' and 'Variegata'. *A. victoriae-reginae*, which has dull green, white-edged, triangular leaves, is one of the best to grow indoors.
Light Bright/filtered.
Temperature Cool to warm.

Watering and feeding Keep moist when in growth and reduce watering in winter. Never let the potting compost become waterlogged. Apply a liquid fertilizer occasionally during the summer.
Cultivation Pot on in spring, using a free-draining, slightly acid potting compost with some added grit and sand.

Allium schoenoprasum
Chives

This member of the onion family is an attractive plant, with purple or white flowers, as well as being edible. The hollow leaves can be used in salads.
Light Bright/filtered.
Temperature Cool to warm.
Watering and feeding Water freely when in growth and sparingly during winter. Apply a balanced liquid fertilizer from spring to autumn.

Cultivation Divide bulbous clumps and pot up in a loam-based potting compost with some added sharp sand.

Alocasia
Elephant's ear plant

These plants are perfect for creating a tropical mood. The spectacular giant taro (*A. macrorrhiza*) needs high humidity and warmth, so a conservatory is ideal. The dark green leaves of the kris plant (*A. sanderiana*) have silver veining and a metallic sheen.
Light Bright/indirect.
Temperature Warm/humid.
Watering and feeding Water freely and feed monthly when in growth. Water moderately in winter.
Cultivation Grow this plant in loam-based potting compost.

Aloe ferox

This succulent is green with red-tinged spikes, perfect colouring for autumn.

Spectacular scarlet-orange flowers are usually produced in summer.
Light Bright/filtered.
Temperature Average room.
Watering and feeding Water moderately through the year, but sparingly when dormant. Feed occasionally in summer.
Cultivation Grow in a loam-based potting compost (soil mix) with sharp sand or grit to aid drainage.

Aloysia triphylla
Lemon verbena
This is the most wonderful lemon-scented herb, with lance-shaped leaves on long graceful stems.
Light Bright/filtered.
Temperature Cool.
Watering and feeding Water freely when in growth, but do not allow to become waterlogged. Apply a liquid fertilizer during flowering.
Cultivation Grow in a light, free-draining potting compost. Take softwood

cuttings in spring or semi-hardwood cuttings in late summer.

Anigozanthos flavidus
Kangaroo paw
Although it flowers in spring and summer when grown outside, in a conservatory it can bloom all year round. The flowers are orange.
Light Bright/filtered.
Temperature Average room.
Watering and feeding Water freely and feed monthly when in growth. Water sparingly in winter.
Cultivation Grow in loam-based potting compost with added sand.

Begonia
Foliage begonias are attractive all year round and make good conservatory plants. The leaves of *B. rex* hybrids are brightly variegated in shades of green, silver, brown, red, pink and purple. The leaves of *B.* 'Norah Bedson', a

hybrid of *B. bowerae*, are blotched brown and green. Cane-like species, such as *B.* 'Mrs Hashimoto', are good for conservatories since they have erect or semi-erect stems that do not branch easily.
Light Bright/indirect.
Temperature Cool room.
Watering and feeding Water freely and apply a balanced liquid fertilizer at every second watering when in growth. Water sparingly in winter.
Cultivation Pot on annually in spring in a good-quality loam-based potting compost.

Bougainvillea glabra
This vigorous climber has clusters of floral bracts in white, pink and purple.
Light Bright/filtered.
Temperature Warm.
Watering and feeding Water freely and apply a balanced liquid fertilizer monthly when in growth. Water sparingly in winter.

Cultivation In early spring, top-dress large containers or, if necessary, repot in a loam-based potting compost.

Campanula isophylla
Falling stars
This trailing plant has bell-shaped, blue flowers. It can be grown indoors for a while, but a conservatory is better.
Light Bright/filtered.
Temperature Cool/average.
Watering and feeding Water freely and apply a balanced fertilizer monthly when in growth. Keep moist in winter.
Cultivation Pot on annually in spring, using a loam-based compost.

Capsicum annuum Grossum Group
Sweet or bell peppers
The heavy red or green fruits are borne on quite delicate stems and will

Aloysia triphylla

Begonia 'Norah Bedson'

Bougainvillea glabra

Capsicum annuum Grossum Group

need staking as they ripen. Peppers require plenty of warmth in order to ripen; they make good conservatory plants, or they can be grown on a sunny windowsill. Pinch out the tips of young plants to encourage a good bushy habit.
Light Bright/filtered.
Temperature Warm (above 21°C/70°F).
Watering and feeding Water freely and apply a balanced liquid fertilizer every two weeks when in growth until the fruit starts to colour.
Cultivation Grow new from seed in early spring each year.

Capsicum annuum Longum Group
Chilli pepper
The conical chilli peppers are held upright on bushy plants. The fruits turn from green to purple to red.
Light Bright/indirect.
Temperature Warm/humid.

Watering and feeding Water freely when in growth and sparingly in winter. Apply a balanced liquid fertilizer every two weeks when in growth until the fruits start to colour, then stop.
Cultivation Grow in loam-based potting compost (soil mix).

Citrus
Both oranges and lemons are probably natives of northern India, certainly China, and are thought to have been brought to the West by Arab traders via North Africa, Arabia and Syria, thence to Spain and Sicily. As their origins suggest, citrus plants are tender and must be protected from frost in temperate regions. However, they actually prefer cool rather than hot conditions. If they are grown in temperate climates, with cold, frosty winters, they can be kept outdoors during the summer, but

must be brought indoors to a temperate conservatory in the winter.

The glossy evergreen leaves of the lemon tree (*C. limon*) set off the small white flowers beautifully. The fruit takes a long time to ripen and, in fact, the plant will probably not produce fruit until it has grown into a small tree with mature root growth. Bitter Seville oranges (*C. aurantium*), along with other citrus fruits, are beautiful, exotic plants for a conservatory. Most citrus trees may reach a height of approximately 1.8–3m/ 6–10ft if they are grown in a conservatory.
Light Bright/filtered.
Temperature Cool to warm; they hate draughts.
Watering and feeding Water freely when in growth, allowing the potting compost to partially dry out before watering again, and in winter reduce watering to a minimum. Mist daily

when in growth and apply a balanced liquid fertilizer every three weeks.
Cultivation Pot on, if need be, in spring, using a loam-based potting compost, or top-dress with fresh potting compost.

Clerodendrum myricoides 'Ugandense'
Blue glory bower
This evergreen climber from West Africa is best grown in a conservatory. It has blue to purple flowers with long lower 'lips'. The winding stems can be trained around a hoop. *C. thomsoniae* can be grown indoors, but also prefers a conservatory. It has dark green, heart-shaped leaves and red and white flowers in summer.
Light Bright/indirect.
Temperature Warm.
Watering and feeding Water freely and apply a balanced liquid fertilizer monthly when in growth. Water sparingly in winter.

Capsicum annuum Longum Group

Citrus limon

Clerodendrum thomsoniae

Clivia miniata

Colchicum autumnale

Coriandrum sativum

Cyclamen

Cymbidium

Cultivation When pot-bound, pot on in loam-based potting compost (soil mix). Dead-head regularly to produce more flowers.

Clivia
Kaffir lily
These evergreen perennials have fleshy, rhizomatous roots. *C. miniata* has strap-shaped leaves and attractive large flowerheads of funnel-shaped, orange or yellow flowers in early spring.
Light Bright/filtered.
Temperature Average room.
Watering and feeding Water moderately when in growth, but sparingly in winter until the flower stalk is at least 15cm/6in tall. Feed occasionally from flowering time until early autumn.
Cultivation Pot on when it becomes pot-bound, as soon as flowering is over, in a loam-based potting compost.

Colchicum
Autumn crocus
These corms are known as naked ladies because they flower in early autumn before the leaves emerge. *C. autumnale* has large, crocus-shaped flowers, in shades of pink. The corms and leaves are poisonous.
Light Bright/filtered.
Temperature Cool.
Watering and feeding Water moderately.
Cultivation Grow in good-quality loam-based potting compost. Place in a light position and leave to flower. Plant outside after flowering, if you like.

Coriandrum sativum
Coriander (cilantro)
This Mediterranean herb has cut leaves and heads of small white flowers. It is not a very attractive plant, but it imparts a distinctive flavour to food. It is grown for its seeds, and the lower leaves are popular in a range of dishes. It is also

used as a garnish. The leaves can be picked during the growing season.
Light Bright/filtered.
Temperature Cool room.
Watering and feeding Water freely when in growth, but do not allow to become waterlogged. Apply a half-strength balanced liquid fertilizer when in growth.
Cultivation Grow from seed in pots each year in a good-quality loam-based potting compost with some added grit to improve drainage.

Cyclamen
It is the florists' cyclamen derived from *C. persicum* that is usually grown in conservatories. It is available in a range of sizes and colours, including pinks, reds, purples, salmon and white. The petals may be frilled or ruffled. The leaves are often marbled with white or silver. It can flower from autumn to early spring.

Light Bright/indirect.
Temperature Cool to warm.
Watering and feeding Water freely when in growth, reducing the amount after flowering. Keep dry during the resting period. Feed every two weeks when growing and flowering.
Cultivation Grow in a good-quality loam-based potting compost, enriched with leaf mould and some added grit. Keep dry when the plant is dormant, repot in autumn and water to restart growth.

Cymbidium
A genus of around 45 species, including epiphytes and semi-terrestrial orchids, there are a great many hybrids, most of which are grown indoors. Plants have upright spikes of large waxy-looking flowers, ranging from green and yellow to pink and white, many of which are speckled. Most are good

Dicksonia fibrosa

Dracaena sanderiana

Dudleya pulverulenta

Echeveria

for cool conservatories, although they do require good ventilation and are delicate, so need to be in a position where they won't be knocked.
Light Bright/indirect.
Temperature Cool to warm; they require good ventilation.
Watering and feeding Water freely in spring and summer, sparingly in autumn and winter. Never let the roots dry out. Feed during the flowering period.
Cultivation Repot only when the existing pot is full of roots, and use a special orchid compost (soil mix).

Dicksonia
Tree fern
D. fibrosa is a dramatic fern, with beautiful curls on the new fronds, a good specimen plant for a cool conservatory. Many of the tree ferns sold at garden centres are *D. antarctica*, which is bought as a log rather than in a pot. The

log should be soaked thoroughly first and then put in a pot that is deep enough to stabilize the plant, and no more.
They will grow up to 2.1m/7ft under glass. There are roots in the fibrous mass of old leaf bases, but it will probably take a year for the cut log to form new roots. During this time, keep the trunk moist. Some growers recommend watering the crown as well. Tree ferns can also be put outdoors during summer, where they bring an exotic atmosphere to a patio.
Light Bright/filtered.
Temperature Cool/humid.
Watering and feeding Water the trunk so that it is constantly damp and apply a high-nitrogen liquid fertilizer monthly.
Cultivation Pot on when roots appear in the drainage holes of the container, using a loam-

based potting compost with added bark, charcoal and leaf mould.

Dracaena
These palm-like plants have striking variegation and a bold outline, which looks impressive in modern conservatories. *D. sanderiana* has oval to lance-shaped leaves, edged with a broad creamy-white band. *D. marginata* has narrow green leaves, edged with purplish red. More good, brightly coloured varieties include 'Colorama' and 'Tricolor'.
Light Bright/indirect.
Temperature Cool to warm.
Watering and feeding Water freely and apply a balanced liquid fertilizer monthly when in growth. Water sparingly in winter. Never let the roots dry out.
Cultivation Repot in spring if necessary in good-quality loam-based potting compost.

Dudleya pulverulenta
This rosette-forming succulent is a delicate greenish grey. The tapering leaves emerge from a thick stem. Red to yellow, star-shaped flowers may appear in spring or early summer.
Light Bright/filtered.
Temperature Warm.
Watering and feeding Water moderately and apply a half-strength balanced liquid fertilizer monthly when in growth. Keep barely moist in summer when the plant is semi-dormant.
Cultivation Pot on in spring, using cactus potting compost.

Echeveria
These rosette-forming succulents are grown for their attractive shape and colouring – many have red-tipped leaves, and some form a thick stalk with the rosette at the top. Most produce pink, yellow or red flowers on tall stalks arising

from the leaf axils. There are many species and hybrids.

E. elegans has fleshy, bluish-white leaves, up to 15cm/6in across. Pink or red flowers, tipped with yellow, appear from early spring to mid-summer. *E.* 'Perle von Nürnberg' has grey-pink colouring.
Light Bright/filtered.
Temperature Average room.
Watering and feeding Water moderately when in growth and keep just moist in winter. Avoid getting water on the leaves as this may damage their waxy layer and lead to rotting. Apply a half-strength balanced liquid fertilizer monthly when in growth.
Cultivation Pot on in spring, using a standard cactus potting compost (soil mix).

Elymus hispidus
Wheatgrass
The bright green young shoots of wheatgrass resemble a perfect indoor lawn. Providing you keep clipping the shoots, a tray of wheatgrass will last for some time. The leaf blades are used for juicing.
Light Bright/indirect.
Temperature Cool.
Watering and feeding Water freely when in growth, but do not allow to become waterlogged.
Cultivation It is best to grow new plants from seed. Sprinkle the seed on a thin layer of potting compost in a tray, water, and then put into a warm dark cupboard until it starts to sprout. As soon as this happens, place in a bright room where the 'lawn' will burst into life.

Eucomis autumnalis
Pineapple lily
This late-flowering bulb is ideal for a cool conservatory. It has tiny, green-white flowers, topped with a tuft of bracts. *E. bicolor* has pale green flowers with purple-margined bracts.
Light Bright/filtered.
Temperature Average room.
Watering and feeding Water freely when in growth and sparingly when dormant.
Cultivation Keep the bulb dry over winter and then plant 10–15cm (4–6in) below the surface of loam-based potting compost with added grit.

Ficus
Fig
The fig plants used as houseplants are grown for their foliage. The common fig (*F. carica*) can grow up to 2.1m/7ft in the home, but a younger plant looks spectacular displayed on a plinth. *F. binnendijkii* 'Alii' is an evergreen that enjoys being indoors. The long, shiny, elliptical leaves are held on slender elegant branches. The weeping fig (*F. benjamina*) can grow to 1.5m/5ft given the right conditions and is one of the most effective plants for purifying the air. The creeping fig (*F. pumila*) is a delicate, evergreen, trailing climber that looks good growing underneath larger specimens. Figs may lose their leaves if shocked by draughts, lack of water or being moved.
Light Bright/filtered.
Temperature Warm, average room.
Watering and feeding Water freely when in growth (large plants will need frequent watering as the larger area of the leaves loses water faster). Feed monthly with a high-nitrogen liquid fertilizer when in growth. Figs respond well to feeding.
Cultivation When pot-bound, pot on using a loam-based potting compost with added bark.

Fortunella japonica
Kumquat
Although the kumquat looks like a member of the citrus family, it belongs

Elymus hispidus

Eucomis autumnalis

Ficus benjamina

Fortunella japonica

to a different genus. It is a small, compact, attractive tree which makes an ideal conservatory plant. The glossy evergreen leaves set off the small white flowers to perfection, and the egg-shaped fruits that follow are a lovely bright orange-yellow. They ripen in autumn and winter. Frozen kumquats can be used to make wonderfully exotic ice cubes in summer drinks.
Light Bright/filtered.
Temperature Cool to warm; it hates draughts.
Watering and feeding Water freely when in growth, allowing the potting compost (soil mix) to partially dry out before watering again, and in winter reduce watering to a minimum. Mist daily when in growth and apply a balanced liquid fertilizer every three weeks or so.
Cultivation Pot on, if necessary, in spring, using a loam-based potting compost, or top-dress with fresh potting compost. Try growing kumquats from pips (seeds).

Fragaria vesca
Alpine strawberry
The strawberry is a creeping perennial with pretty, white flowers that have yellow centres. The delicious small fruit has tiny yellow seeds embedded in the surface.

F. vesca has smaller, but more aromatic, fruits that can be eaten fresh or used in a range of desserts, conserves and juices.
Light Bright/filtered.
Temperature Cool.
Watering and feeding Water the plant freely when it is in growth but do not allow the compost to become waterlogged. Apply a liquid fertilizer weekly during flowering.
Cultivation Remove side runners between spring and autumn, and pot on the plant in a good-quality loam-based potting compost, as required.

Gardenia augusta 'Veitchiana'
The shiny leaves contrast beautifully with the double, white, short-lived flowers.
Light Bright/indirect.
Temperature Cool to average.
Watering and feeding Water freely and apply a balanced liquid fertilizer monthly when in growth. Water sparingly in winter. Use soft or demineralized water and never let the roots dry out.
Cultivation Repot the plant in spring, using an ericaceous (lime-free) potting compost.

Guzmania lingulata
These exotic bromeliads, mainly from the tropical rainforests of South America, are usually grown for their showy bracts. Dark green, lance-shaped leaves form a funnel that holds water. The flower stalk is topped by red or orange bracts that wrap around tiny, yellowish-white flowers.
Light Bright/filtered.
Temperature Very warm/humid (think Andean rainforest). Provide cooler conditions in winter.
Watering and feeding When in growth, water moderately, filling the rosette centres. Water sparingly in winter. No feeding is required.
Cultivation Grow in bromeliad potting compost. Guzmanias have such small root systems that they rarely need repotting.

Hibiscus rosa-sinensis
Rose of China
This is the only species in the genus that is grown as an indoor plant. It has beautiful single or double

Fragaria vesca

Gardenia augusta

Guzmania lingulata

Hibiscus rosa-sinensis

Hedychium

Hippeastrum hybrid

Hyacinthus orientalis

Impatiens hybrid

flowers, with stamens on a central column. Colours include red, pink, orange, yellow and white.
Light Bright/filtered.
Temperature Warm.
Watering and feeding Water freely when in growth and sparingly in winter, but never let the roots dry out. Apply a balanced liquid fertilizer monthly in summer.
Cultivation Pot on in late spring, using a loam-based potting compost (soil mix).

Hedychium
Ginger lily
Grown for its dense head of pretty scented flowers, the ginger lily makes a wonderful addition to the conservatory, where it will thrive in the warm conditions. *H. coronarium* (white butterfly ginger) produces pink, orange or red tubular flowers on terminal spikes in late summer, which have the most wonderful fragrance,

almost like gardenias. It requires a large pot to flower well.
Light Bright/indirect.
Temperature Warm.
Watering and feeding Water freely all year round and feed monthly with a balanced fertilizer.
Cultivation Grow in good-quality loam-based potting compost.

Hippeastrum hybrids
Often incorrectly known as amaryllis, this bulb is usually forced to flower in late winter, especially for Christmas. It is found in a range of colours, including white, pink and red.
Light Bright/filtered.
Temperature Cool room.
Watering and feeding Water moderately when the bulbs are growing; keep the soil almost dry when the plant is resting. Feed every two weeks with a balanced liquid fertilizer once the leaves start to grow.

Cultivation Bulbs prepared for winter flowering should be planted when available. Unprepared bulbs flower later. Bulbs planted in late winter or early spring will flower in mid- or late spring. A soil temperature of 21°C/70°F is required to start dormant bulbs into growth. Pot up, burying only about half the bulb. When the stalk reaches 15cm/6in, keep in a light position. Cut off the stalk when blooming is over. Reduce watering in early autumn and allow the leaves to die back. Keep in a conservatory, or outdoors in summer. Start into growth again by resuming watering a month or two later.

Hyacinthus orientalis
Hyacinth
The pink, blue or white flowers are held on a single stem. Use specially prepared bulbs for forcing

indoors; plant in a cool, dark place initially and bring into the light only when shoots emerge. Keep in a cool place until they flower, then move to a warmer location.
Light Bright/indirect.
Temperature Cool.
Watering and feeding Water moderately when in growth.
Cultivation Grow in humus-rich compost. Discard or plant outside after flowering.

Impatiens hybrids
Busy Lizzie
Masses of flat flowers appear at any time of the year if the temperature is maintained above 16°C/60°F. Blooms are mostly in shades of red, orange, pink and white, of which many are often multi-coloured and sometimes double. The flowers of the New Guinea Group are usually fewer but larger.
Light Bright/indirect.

Isolepsis cernua

Jasminum polyanthum

Kalanchoe thyrsiflora

Lilium hybrid

Temperature Cool to average; humid.
Watering and feeding Water freely and feed every two weeks when in growth. Water sparingly in winter.
Cultivation Repot in spring if necessary. They are easy to grow, so raise new plants from cuttings or seed and discard if they become leggy.

Isolepis cernua
Club rush
This indoor grass, formerly known as *Scirpus cernuus*, is fresh and green and makes an interesting statement in a conservatory.
Light Bright/indirect.
Temperature Average/humid.
Watering and feeding Water freely when the plant is in growth. Water sparingly in winter. Apply a balanced fertilizer monthly when in growth.
Cultivation Grow in a loam-based potting compost (soil mix).

Jasminum polyanthum
Jasmine
This pretty evergreen conservatory climber bears a mass of white flowers in late winter or early spring.
Light Bright/indirect.
Temperature Cool to warm.
Watering and feeding Water freely and apply a low-nitrogen liquid fertilizer monthly when the plant is in growth. Water sparingly in winter.
Cultivation Grow in good-quality loam-based potting compost.

Kalanchoe thyrsiflora
The pale green, oval leaves of this bushy, white-frosted succulent have smudged red margins. It produces panicles of little yellow flowers in spring. The whole plant looks like a flower made from marzipan.
Light Bright/filtered.
Temperature Warm, dry, average room.

Watering and feeding Water moderately and apply a balanced liquid fertilizer monthly when the plant is in growth. Water sparingly in winter. Do not splash the leaves with water because it will mark them.
Cultivation Pot on at any time of year, using a good-quality loam-based potting compost with added grit in order to improve drainage.

Lilium hybrids
Lily
The bulbs in this genus that are grown as pot plants are usually hybrids. They have become popular indoor plants with the introduction of compact varieties. Most hybrids have trumpet-shaped or backward curving petals in shades of red, orange, yellow and white, usually spotted, mottled, or flushed with another colour. 'Casa Blanca' is a white variety.

Light Bright/filtered.
Temperature Cool to average.
Watering and feeding Water freely and apply a high-potash liquid fertilizer every few weeks when the plant is in growth.
Cultivation Bulbs are usually planted in a loam-based potting compost in autumn or mid- to late winter, depending on when they are available. Keep the bulbs in a cool, dry place, with the soil just moist. When the buds show colour, move to a warmer room, but avoid high temperatures, which will shorten the life of the blooms. Plant outside after flowering, if you like.

Lithops
Living stone, stone plant
These intriguing, dwarf, stemless succulents from southern Africa look like greenish-brown stones with a smooth surface. The pairs of fused, swollen leaves

grow into small clumps. The pairs of leaves part to produce a single flower in late summer.

Many species are available, but you are most likely to find *L. bella*, which has brownish-yellow, fused leaves with depressed, darker patches. White, daisy-like flowers appear in late summer or early autumn. Planted in a shallow tray that is top-dressed with gravel and small stones, it is difficult to distinguish the real stones from the living ones.
Light Bright/filtered.
Temperature Warm, dry, average room.
Watering and feeding Water with great care, only moderately in summer and not at all in winter. Start watering again when the new leaves appear. Feeding is seldom necessary, but if the plant has been in the same pot for many years, feed occasionally with a cactus fertilizer.

Cultivation Grow in cactus potting compost (soil mix) with added leaf mould.

Lycopersicon esculentum
Tomato
Dwarf bushy varieties of tomato are available which can be grown indoors. 'Minibel' and 'Tumbler' are both excellent varieties. Apply a thick mulch of organic matter to help retain moisture.
Light Bright/filtered.
Temperature Warm.
Watering and feeding Water freely when in growth and apply a proprietary tomato feed every two weeks.
Cultivation Grow from seed or buy young plants and treat them as annuals.

Mammillaria zeilmanniana
These cacti are undemanding plants for year-round interest and

will make you smile. The clustering round stems produce white, hair-like spines that are tempting to touch, but don't, as you will damage them. They may flower in summer.
Light Bright/filtered.
Temperature Warm.
Watering and feeding Water moderately and apply a balanced liquid fertilizer monthly in summer. Keep almost dry in winter.
Cultivation Grow the plant in standard cactus potting compost.

Mandevilla X amoena 'Alice du Pont'
This twining conservatory climber has funnel-shaped, pink flowers. The milky sap can irritate the skin.
Light Bright/filtered.
Temperature Warm (min. 10–15°C/50–59°F).
Watering and feeding Water moderately and apply a balanced liquid

fertilizer monthly when in growth. Water less during winter.
Cultivation Pot on in spring, using a loam-based potting compost with some added grit.

Mentha
Mint
Mint is a large family of highly fragrant, flowering plants that have been used for centuries for their culinary and medicinal properties. Although there are many diverse species available, most are more suitable for garden use.

However, two mints make suitable windowsill or indoor plants. They are Corsican or rock mint (*M. requienii*), which is a mat-forming, semi-evergreen species, with a very strong scent, and creeping pennyroyal (*M. pulegium*). The latter is said to deter ants, so it is doubly useful indoors. Both varieties are low spreaders with mauve-

Lithops

Lycopersicon esculentum

Mandevilla x amoena 'Alice du Pont'

Mentha

purple flowers, but they have different cultivation requirements so you need to read the label.
Light *M. requienii*: shade; *M. pulegium*: bright/filtered.
Temperature Cool to warm.
Watering and feeding *M. requienii*: water freely when in growth and keep moist at all times; *M. pulegium*: water freely when in growth, but do not allow to become waterlogged. It needs a very free-draining potting compost (soil mix).
Cultivation Grow in a loam-based potting compost, with added grit for drainage.
Warning *M. pulegium* should not be eaten during pregnancy.

Monstera deliciosa
Swiss cheese plant
This climber has thick stems and aerial roots. Large, attractive leaves, up to 60cm/2ft across, are entire and heart-shaped initially, but become incised and perforated with age. There is also a variegated variety. Pretty white lily-like flowers sometimes appear on plants that are grown in conservatories. It can grow to ceiling height, so allow plenty of room.
Light Bright/filtered.
Temperature Warm.
Watering and feeding Water freely from spring to autumn, but sparingly in winter. Mist the leaves regularly.
Cultivation Requires a suitable climbing support, such as a moss-covered pole. Lightly sponge the leaves occasionally.

Musa acuminata 'Dwarf Cavendish'
Banana
The evergreen, paddle-shaped leaves of this plant are huge, but damage easily. The plant can grow up to 2.1m/7ft in the home, so allow adequate room. It may flower and produce fruit in a conservatory.
Light Bright/filtered.
Temperature Warm/humid.
Watering and feeding Water freely, applying a balanced liquid fertilizer each time, when in growth. Water sparingly in winter.
Cultivation The large leaves will need a heavy pot to steady them. Grow in loam-based potting compost and pot up the suckers that appear at the base of the plant if you wish to propagate.

Myrtus communis
Myrtle
This evergreen tree has glossy, dark green leaves, up to 5cm/2in long. In mid- to late summer saucer-shaped, creamy flowers almost hide the foliage, followed in autumn by small black berries.
Light Full sun.
Temperature Warm.
Watering and feeding Grow in moisture-retentive but well-drained compost.
Cultivation Apply a 5–7cm/2–3in mulch of well-rotted garden compost or manure around the base of the plant in early spring. Remove any unwanted growth in late spring.

Narcissus
Daffodil
Daffodils herald the arrival of spring and add vibrant colour to a conservatory. *N.* 'Tête-à-Tête' is a dwarf daffodil with golden yellow flowers. The paper-white narcissus (*N. papyraceus*) has strongly scented white flowers that will fill a conservatory with perfume. 'Ziva' is suitable for forcing.
Light Bright/indirect.
Temperature Cool.
Watering and feeding Water moderately when in growth indoors. Continue watering often if replanting outside.

Musa acuminata

Myrtus communis

Narcissus papyraceus

Nepenthes 'Director G. T. Moore'

Nertera granadensis

Ocimum basilicum

Olea europaea

Paphiopedilum hybrid

Cultivation Plant new bulbs in autumn in a loam-based potting compost (soil mix) in a cool dark place. When shoots appear, bring into a warmer room. Plant old bulbs in the garden where they will do well.

Nepenthes
Monkey cup, tropical pitcher plant
The leaves of these carnivorous plants have a midrib that extends in the form of a tendril to become a hollow 'pitcher', ranging in colour from pale yellow to green or purple-red.
Light Bright/filtered.
Temperature Hot/humid (min. 18°C/64°F).
Watering and feeding Water freely. Apply a high-nitrogen liquid fertilizer weekly.
Cultivation Grow in a potting compost made from two parts bark, two parts perlite and one part peat-substitute.

Nertera granadensis
Bead plant
These plants have tiny, bead-like, orange fruits and mat-forming leaves.
Light Bright/indirect.
Temperature Cool, average room/humid.
Watering and feeding Water freely and apply a balanced liquid fertilizer monthly when in growth. Water sparingly in winter.
Cultivation Grow this plant in a loam-free potting compost.

Ocimum basilicum
Basil
This herb has pungent, green leaves. The purple-leaved variety, 'Purple Ruffles', has pink flowers. Pinch out the leaves from the top to encourage bushing out.
Light Bright/filtered.
Temperature Warm.
Watering and feeding Water moderately. Likes dry heat and dislikes humidity. Apply a liquid fertilizer monthly when in growth.

Cultivation It is probably best to grow new plants from seed. They like a rich loam-based potting compost with some added grit or sharp sand for extra drainage.

Olea europaea
Olive
This evergreen tree has an elegant form and is ideal for a conservatory. It has silvery green leaves and little white flowers, followed by pale green fruit that eventually turns black.
Light Bright/filtered.
Temperature Cool.
Watering and feeding Water moderately and apply a balanced liquid fertilizer monthly when in growth. Water the plant sparingly in winter.
Cultivation Grow in a loam-based potting compost with some sharp sand added for free drainage. Top-dress especially large specimens in their pots every year.

Opuntia
This is a large genus of more than 200 cacti, ranging from low ground-cover to tree-sized plants, many popular with collectors. The prickly pear (*O. ficus-indica*) is one of the most well-loved and sculptural of cacti, with its fascinating collection of prickly discs. The bristles can become lodged in the skin and are then difficult to remove.
Light Bright/filtered.
Temperature Warm.
Watering and feeding Water moderately when in growth and sparingly during winter. Apply a fertilizer formulated for cacti a few times in summer.
Cultivation Grow this plant in standard cactus potting compost.

Paphiopedilum hybrids
Slipper orchid
These winter-flowering evergreen orchids make attractive houseplants.

Passiflora

Pelargonium 'Lord Bute'

Phalaenopsis hybrid

Phoenix canariensis

P. parishii has twisted, brown-spotted, green-tinged petals, which are pendulous, and a greenish-brown pouch.
Light Partial shade.
Temperature Cool to average; likes humidity.
Watering and feeding Water freely and apply an orchid fertilizer every three to four weeks when in growth. Mist daily. Water sparingly in winter.
Cultivation Enjoys being pot-bound, but, if potting on, use a terrestrial orchid potting compost (soil mix).

Passiflora
Passion flower
There are a huge number of different species of these stunning climbing plants, which have distinctive colourful flowers and a wonderful scent. The attractive fruits are usually yellow, and some of the indoor varieties are good to eat. *P.* 'Lady Margaret' is a hybrid of *P. coccinea* and *P. incarnata*, a fast-growing

vine with intense red/pink sepals and petals, a white centre and white-tipped corona. *P. quadrangularis* (giant grandadilla) is another fast-growing species, and produces giant green to yellow fruit.
Light Full sun or partial shade.
Temperature Warm/humid.
Watering and feeding Keep compost moist at all times and feed throughout summer with a high potash liquid feed or in spring with a controlled-release fertilizer.
Cultivation Likes loamy compost; dislikes alkaline compost. Hand-pollinate with pollen from a flower that has been open for over 12 hours to pollinate a newly opened flower.

Pelargonium
Grown for their colourful flowers or scented leaves, pelargoniums are ideal for a sunny windowsill or conservatory. There are

different groups in a range of colours, including regal (single flowers in single or combined shades of red, pink, purple, orange, white or reddish black); ivy-leaved (single to double flowers in shades of red, pink, mauve, purple or white); and zonal (single or double flowers in shades of scarlet, purple, pink, white, orange and rarely yellow).

As well as their showy flowers, pelargoniums have attractive leaves, large, bold and round or small and ivy-shaped. Good regal varieties include 'Carisbrooke' (pink and red), 'Lord Bute' (red and black) and 'Sefton' (cerise and red).

Scented-leaved pelargoniums have small, single flowers in shades of mauve, pink, purple or white, and are largely grown for the strong aromas that are released when you brush against the leaves. Scented species

include *P. capitatum* and *P. graveolens* (rose-scented); *P. crispum* (lemon-scented); and *P. tomentosum* (peppermint-scented).
Light Bright/filtered.
Temperature Warm.
Watering and feeding Water moderately, applying a balanced liquid fertilizer every two weeks when in growth. Water sparingly in winter.
Cultivation Pot on in loam-based potting compost. Cut back in late winter/early spring. Dead-head often.

Phalaenopsis hybrids
Moth orchid
These evergreen orchids are ideal for a warm conservatory. The arching stems of flowers will last for months, and may appear more than once a year. *P. Allegria* is a white variety.
Light Bright/indirect; no direct sun.
Temperature Warm/humid.

Watering and feeding
Water freely, preferably with rainwater, when in growth and sparingly in winter. Mist daily. Apply an orchid fertilizer monthly when in growth.
Cultivation Likes to be pot-bound. If potting on, use an epiphytic orchid compost (soil mix).

Phoenix canariensis
Canary Island palm
Most of the plants in this genus of palms will become small trees outdoors, but some make attractive conservatory plants when young. This species has feathery fronds, stiff and erect at first, arching later, with narrow leaflets.
Light Bright/filtered.
Temperature Average room.
Watering and feeding
Water moderately and apply a balanced liquid fertilizer monthly when it is in growth. Water sparingly in winter.

Cultivation Pot on only when the plant becomes pot-bound as it dislikes its roots being disturbed.

Plumbago auriculata
Cape leadwort
This evergreen conservatory climber from South Africa has clusters of pale blue flowers. There is a white variety, *P. a.* var. *alba*.
Light Bright/filtered.
Temperature Cool to warm.
Watering and feeding
Water freely when in growth and sparingly in winter. Apply a balanced liquid fertilizer every two weeks in spring and summer.
Cultivation Pot on in the spring, using a loam-based potting compost.

Primula obconica
Poison primrose
Contact with the pale green leaves irritates the skin. Pink, white or blue flowers appear in winter and spring.

Light Bright/indirect.
Temperature Cool.
Watering and feeding
Water freely when in growth and sparingly in winter. Apply a half-strength liquid fertilizer once a week when in flower.
Cultivation Pot on in loam-based potting compost with added grit or perlite.

Prunus armeniaca 'Aprigold'
Aprigold apricot
This dwarf apricot has deciduous green foliage and single white flowers. It grows up to 1.8m/6ft. It may bear succulent fruit in a warm conservatory.
Light Full sun.
Temperature Warm.
Watering and feeding
Water only when the compost has dried out and fertilize regularly.
Cultivation Plant in humus-rich, well-drained compost and put outside in summer.

Prunus persica
Peach and nectarine
P. persica 'Bonanza' is a dwarf peach with beautiful flowers and compact form. The dwarf nectarine *P. persica* 'Nectarella' will reach a maximum height of 1.2–1.75m/4–5ft and will produce abundant fruit.
Light Full sun.
Temperature Warm.
Watering and feeding
Water only when the compost has dried out and fertilize regularly.
Cultivation Plant in humus-rich, well-drained compost and put outside during warm summers.

Rebutia fiebrigii
These cacti originate from northern Argentina and parts of Bolivia. This species is a compact plant with dark green, clustering stems, bearing white, red-tinged, hooked spines. Yellow-brown or reddish-orange flowers appear in summer, and they are often grown for these flowers.

Plumbago auriculata

Primula obconica

Prunus persica

Rebutia fiebrigii

Light Bright/filtered.
Temperature
Average/low humidity.
Watering and feeding
Water moderately when
in growth and keep almost
dry at other times. Apply
a weak fertilizer, or one
formulated for cacti, a
few times in summer.
Cultivation Grow in
standard cactus potting
compost (soil mix).

Rosmarinus officinalis
Rosemary
The leaves of this aromatic
evergreen herb from the
Mediterranean make it an
attractive visitor indoors,
perhaps to decorate an
informal dining table, but
it is really a garden plant.
Light Full sun.
Temperature Cool room.
Watering and feeding
They're fairly tolerant but
produce most fragrance if
kept quite dry. They don't
need much feeding.
Cultivation Plant outside
after a brief visit indoors.

Solanum melongena
Aubergine (eggplant)
These delicate plants
respond well to being
indoors, particularly if
they are grown in a warm,
sheltered conservatory.
In cool climates they
are usually grown in a
greenhouse. Although not
the prettiest of plants –
they have sharp prickles
on the backs of the leaves
and tend to look rather
droopy – aubergines are
rewarding to grow for the
attractive fruits.

Good varieties include
'Kermit' and 'Moneymaker'.
The fruits can be stored
for a few weeks after
harvesting in a humid
room. Regularly picking
the fruit will encourage
the production of more.
Light Bright/filtered.
Temperature Warm.
Watering and feeding
Keep well watered and
add a mulch to the surface
of the potting compost
to help retain moisture.

Feed with a balanced
liquid fertilizer every
two weeks.
Cultivation Grow from
seed every year, soaking
the seeds first for a day
or two.

Sparrmannia africana
African hemp
This tree has hairy, heart-
shaped leaves. Small white
flowers appear in summer,
but are often hidden under
the leaves. The leaves look
stunning with light shining
behind them. This plant
will grow up to 2.1m/7ft
tall in the conservatory.
Light Bright/filtered.
Temperature Cool to
warm.
Watering and feeding
Water freely and apply a
balanced liquid fertilizer
monthly from spring.
Water sparingly in winter.
Cultivation When the
plant is pot-bound, pot
on into a heavy pot, using
a good-quality loam-based
potting compost.

Spathiphyllum wallisii
Peace lily
These elegant rhizomatous
evergreen perennials are
grown for their white,
arum-lily-like flowers.
Light Bright/filtered.
Temperature Average.
Watering and feeding
Water freely and apply a
balanced liquid fertilizer
monthly when in growth.
Mist daily. Keep moist
in winter.
Cultivation Grow in
loam-based potting
compost with added grit
for drainage.

Stephanotis floribunda
This lovely conservatory
climber has scented, waxy,
white flowers.
Light Bright/filtered.
Temperature
Average room.
Watering and feeding
Water freely and apply a
balanced liquid fertilizer
every few weeks when in
growth. Mist occasionally.

Rosmarinus officinalis

Solanum melongena

Spathiphyllum wallisii

Stephanotis floribunda

Strelitzia reginae

Streptocarpus 'Albatross'

Tacca chantrieri

Tillandsia cyanea

Cultivation Pot on in spring in a loam-based potting compost (soil mix) with a little extra grit.

Strelitzia reginae
Bird of paradise
Resembling an exotic bird of paradise, the long-lasting, orange and blue flowers sit in a boat-like bract. Only the species described here can be grown as an indoor plant. The main flowering period is spring.
Light Bright/filtered.
Temperature Warm/well-ventilated.
Watering and feeding Water freely and apply a balanced liquid fertilizer monthly when in growth. Water sparingly in winter.
Cultivation Divide and plant root suckers in a loam-based potting compost in spring.

Streptocarpus
Most types of *Streptocarpus* grown in the home are hybrids. These have strap-like leaves 20–30cm/ 8–12in long, growing more or less horizontally. Trumpet-shaped flowers, about 5cm/2in across, are borne on long stems. Flowers are in shades of pink, red and blue, although *S.* 'Albatross' has white ones, and *S.* 'Black Panther' has dark purple blooms.
Light Good, but not direct, light.
Temperature Average.
Watering and feeding Water freely from spring to autumn, but sparingly in winter. Mist the leaves occasionally. Feed regularly in summer.
Cultivation Pot on in spring in a loam-based potting compost.

Tacca chantrieri
Bat flower, devil flower
Weird and beautiful, the flower of this perennial has a complex structure. The green, bell-shaped petals are surrounded by pairs of darker green, or black, floral bracts and hung with long whiskers, thread-like appendages that can reach up to 25cm/10in in length.
Light Partial shade.
Temperature Warm/humid.
Watering and feeding Water freely throughout the year. In summer, mist regularly and apply a half-strength foliar feed monthly.
Cultivation Pot on every few years as necessary, using equal parts coarse bark and leaf mould, with slow-release fertilizer.

Tillandsia cyanea
Members of this genus are air plants, but those grown for their flowers can also be grown in pots. *T. cyanea* has pink, paddle-shaped bracts, edged with purple petals.
Light Bright/indirect.
Temperature Warm/humid.
Watering and feeding Water freely when in growth, ideally with rainwater, and sparingly in winter. Allow to dry out completely between waterings. Apply a half-strength balanced liquid fertilizer monthly when in growth.
Cultivation This plant is unlikely to become pot-bound. Use special terrestrial bromeliad potting compost to plant up offsets.

Zantedeschia aethiopica
Arum lily
Striking, elegant and easy to grow, the flowers are usually pure white, but deep purple and orange varieties are also available.
Light Bright/indirect.
Temperature Cool room.
Watering and feeding Water flowering plants freely and apply a balanced liquid fertilizer every two weeks. Water sparingly in the winter.
Cultivation Pot on as required in loam-based potting compost.

156

suppliers

INTERNATIONAL

Manufacturers
The internet is the best place to look to find local manufacturers, but here are some of the larger companies and useful websites.

Pilkington Group Ltd
www.pilkington.com
Glass manufacturers

Saint Gobain Glass
www.saint-gobain.com
Glass manufacturers

Apropos Tectonic
www.apropos-conservatories.com
Conservatory manufacturers in the UK

Vale Garden Houses
www.valegardenhouses.com
Conservatory manufacturers in the UK, the Channel Islands, Ireland, Belgium, Denmark and Sweden

www.conservatories.com
On-line directory of conservatory manufacturers in the UK and the USA and general advice

www.conservatoriesonline.com
On-line directory of conservatory manufacturers in the UK, Europe, the USA, Canada and Australia and general advice

Furniture, lighting & fabrics
Ikea
www.ikea.com
Furniture, lighting and accessories

Habitat
www.habitat.net/pws/landing.html
Furniture, lighting and accessories

Sunbrella
www.sunbrella.com
Fade-proof, sun-resistant fabric

The Conran Shop
www.conran.com
Contemporary furniture and home furnishings

Vitra
www.vitra.com
Design-oriented furniture manufacturers

UNITED KINGDOM

Furniture, lighting & fabrics
B&Q
www.diy.com
Lighting, flooring, furniture, painting and decorating, conservatories and plants and more

Carol Sharp Studio
www.carolsharp.co.uk
Photographic images on outdoor canvas and conservatory cushions

Donghia UK Ltd
www.donghia.com
Furniture, textiles, trim, lighting, wallcoverings and accessories

Fine Cell Work
www.finecellwork.co.uk
Bespoke tapestry cushions, rugs and quilts

John Cullen
www.johncullenlighting.co.uk
Lighting for house and garden

O ECOTEXTILES
www.oecotextiles.com
Ethical, non-toxic fabrics

The Cale Schiang Partnership
www.schiang.com
Scandinavian furniture and lighting

Accessories
Capital Garden Products
www.capital-garden.com
Large lightweight pots

Hode Pottery
www.hodepottery.co.uk
Stoneware Mediterranean-feel pots

Homebase
www.homebase.co.uk
Houseplants, composts and accessories

Prêt-à-Pot
www.pret-a-pot.co.uk
Ceramic pots

Plants & seeds

Architectural Plants
www.architecturalplants.com
Architectural plants

Jacques Amand
www.jacquesamand.com
Bulb specialist

Jekka's Herbs
www.jekkasherbfarm.com
Herb seeds

McBean's orchids
www.mcbeansorchids.co.uk
Orchid specialist

Mr Fothergill's Seeds
www.Mr-Fothergills.co.uk
Seed collections

Shrubland Park Nurseries
www.shrublandparknurseries.co.uk
Conservatory plants, including succulents

Swanland Nurseries
www.swanlandnurseries.co.uk
*Houseplants and award-winning
pelargonium collections*

The Palm Centre
www.thepalmcentre.co.uk
*Palm trees, cycads, shrubs, bamboos,
indoor plants, ferns and olive trees*

Thompson & Morgan (UK) Ltd
www.thompson-morgan.com
Seed collections

Blackmoor Estate Ltd
www.blackmoorestate.co.uk
Patio fruit tree collections

UNITED STATES & CANADA

Furniture & accessories

Bitters Co.
www.bittersco.com
Textiles, art and homewares

Kuda
www.kudaimports.com
*Furniture and homewares from
Indonesia, China, India and Thailand*

Pier 1 Imports
www.pier1.com
Furniture and homewares

Smith & Hawken
www.smith-hawken.com
Furniture, homewares and plants

Takashimaya New York
www.takashimaya-ny.com
Artisan-made accessories

Urban Cottage
urbancottage-atlanta.com
Furniture and accessories

Plants & seeds

Indoor Gardening Supplies
www.indoorgardening.com

Burpee Seeds and Plants
www.burpee.com

Mission Hills Nursery
www.missionhillsnursery.com

Molbak's Greenhouse and Nursery
www.molbaks.com

Richters Herb Specialists
www.richters.com

AUSTRALIA & NEW ZEALAND

Furniture & accessories

Freedom Furniture
www.freedomfurniture.com.au
Furniture and homewares

Nest
www.nest.co.nz
*Homewares, furniture, fabrics
and lighting*

Parterre
www.parterre.com.au
Furniture and accessories

Plants & seeds

Australian Seed Company
www.ausseed.com.au

Harmony Garden Centre
www.harmonygc.com.au

Lintons Garden and Home
www.lintons.com.au

index